YOU'RE

MY

FAVORITE

YOU'RE

MY

A

TRUE

STORY

FAVORITE

GINNY PRIEM

CONTENTS

PART ONE

PART TWO

DISCLAIMER

This work is based on a true story and depicts actual events in the life of the author as truthfully as recollection permits and in some cases may include time compression. Occasionally, dialogue consistent with the character or nature of the person speaking may have been supplemented or recreated. All persons within are actual individuals; there are no composite characters. The names and genders of some individuals have been changed to respect their privacy.

This book is dedicated to my dad, my all-time favorite.
(Except page 76 – sorry about that, Dad)

PART

ONE

MEET ME
FOR A
COCKTAIL

I'M GROGGY AND DISORIENTED as the sound of my alarm clock wakes me. My eyes adjust to the darkness in the room as I remember where I am. I'm reminded that I'm in yet another hotel room on another exotic work trip—in Alabama.

I roll out of bed, slide my feet into my slippers so as not to touch my bare feet to the highly-trafficked hotel carpeting, and make my way to the bathroom to get ready for the day. I step out of the shower and brush my teeth while I wait for the steam on the mirror in the poorly ventilated bathroom to dissipate so I can swipe my lids, cheeks, and lips with a touch of color.

After pulling myself together, I walk back into the bedroom to get dressed and gather my belongings for my meeting. I toss my laptop and notebook in my bag before heading downstairs to meet with my customer. I'm on my way to the elevator when

I reach for the call button and feel the vibration from my phone buzzing in my bag. It's Lauren messaging me to check in.

"Hey, what's going on?"

"My travels were pretty rough yesterday. I didn't get to bed until about one a.m. I'm having a hard time getting up and moving," I reply.

Lauren asks, "What time are you getting back today?"

I text back, "I land at 9:37 p.m. What do you have going on today? Anything exciting?"

Lauren doesn't answer my question but responds, "And then you leave again tomorrow?"

"I've got a 6:45 a.m. flight Thursday morning to Seattle for my nephew's wedding," I reply.

After I wrap up my customer meeting and lunch, I go back up to my hotel room to pack my things and change out of my work-appropriate dress and stilettos into some more comfortable travel attire: a long-sleeve black and white striped top, black leggings, a long, black cashmere cardigan sweater, and some black sneakers. I pull my slightly longer than shoulder-length golden hair up into my signature topknot bun. With a touch-up of my lip gloss, I take one final glance over to make sure I look halfway presentable before I head to the lobby for my ride to the airport.

My Uber driver drops me off curbside, and I step inside to ride the escalator up one floor to the security line. At most airports, I can send all of my items straight through the X-ray scanner. Unfortunately, there's no TSA precheck option at this small airport, so I wait in line, observing the less-traveled individuals asking about the 3:1:1 rule. They are confused why they can't bring their thirty-two-ounce aerosol can of Aqua Net in their carry-on.

The older gentleman in front of me makes it through the metal detector with no alarm on the third attempt. *Whew!* I push my plastic bins with my laptop and iPad forward on the belt, hoping that I don't hear the 'random' selection alert as I walk through the detector. *That would be embarrassing.*

After making it through the metal detector unscathed, I gather my things as they come through on the opposite side. I repack my belongings and wheel my dark tan carry-on bag in one hand (a gift from the airline when I had flown one million miles) while checking emails on my phone in the other. I walk past the other business travelers and families sitting and waiting for their flights at their gate.

As I stroll by the single gift shop and the quick-serve restaurant, I glance down at my watch to check the time. I'm still full from lunch, but I'm planning ahead. *When will my next opportunity be to eat?* I browse the limited snack options; pretzels, candy bars, and cheese puffs. None of these unhealthy choices speak to me, so I opt to wait and start walking toward my gate.

My turn to board the plane approaches, and I'm eager to get home to my family. Of course, I'll miss cooking dinner and helping with homework tonight, but I'll cherish the moment when I can tiptoe into their bedroom to kiss their sweet little sleeping faces when I get home.

Looking out the window while sitting in the all-too-familiar blue leather seat near the front of the aircraft, I get another message from Lauren. The flight attendant is making the final overhead announcements as we're nearly ready to push back from the gate.

Lauren, "Hey, it's me again. I know this is a tall order, but is there any chance you could meet for a drink tonight when you land?"

I know something is going on when she asks me to get together for a cocktail when I land, knowing it will be well past ten p.m.

I responded, "I sure could. Where are you thinking?"

Lauren, being considerate of my travels and the time of day, suggests, "Let's meet somewhere close to your house." I appreciate this because we live about twenty minutes apart and I'll have had a long day of travel.

This prompts me to ask, "Is everything ok? I'm excited to see you. How about BLVD or Bacio?"

And then I see the dot dot dot dancing across my screen. Knowing she's typing makes me a little anxious. I begin to wonder how she will respond, a million things running through my mind. It seems like she's crafting a lengthy message as I stare at my phone for an uncomfortably long time when she finally responds with, "Everything will be ok. Just need to catch up. Excited to see you, too. Let's do BLVD *Red Heart Emoji*"

I'm certainly not one opposed to getting together for a cocktail or a few, even if it is on a Tuesday (although I'd consider myself to be more of a wine or champagne gal). However, anything past nine p.m. is the middle of the night to me, especially on a Tuesday.

This feels different. Lauren's never asked for something like this from me before, and we've been friends for about seven years. We get together for workouts and coffee but never for drinks.

When she asks me for this "tall order," I immediately know something's going on. She needs me. So I will race to her side and help her through any situation she's facing.

On this wintry November Tuesday, I walk to my car in the parking ramp at the airport. I get in and let out a deep exhale, which gives way to a misty cloud of condensation, and prepare myself for what's to come. I start the car and don't wait for the engine to completely warm up before putting it in gear.

Before backing out of my parking space, I dial Chad. He answers right away, "Hi Babe."

"Hi Babe. Are the kids in bed?" I ask.

"Yep, they've been sleeping for about an hour."

"Oh good. I can't wait to do my morning breakfast routine with them and get them off to school tomorrow. They are the sweetest in the morning."

"They love their mornings with you, too."

"I'm on my way to meet up with Lauren and should be home by 11:15 since the restaurant closes at eleven."

"Sounds good. I hope everything is okay with Lauren. Tell her I say hi and wake me up when you get home. Emilio and I are excited to see you."

Oddly enough, Emilio can't see or hear me when I walk past him. He's been blind and deaf for several years now. Some might find it disruptive, but I find the sound of the snores coming from his squished face soothing, and I love seeing him curled up like a fluff ball on the floor in his plush dog bed.

"Ok, I will. See you soon," I say.

"Love you, Babe."

"I love you, too."

We hang up, and I drive from the airport to meet Lauren, my hands gripping the cold leather of the steering wheel. Despite the temperature, I can tell through the thin material of my gloves that my hands are sweaty and white-knuckled, partly from feeling cold and partly from the anticipation of what I'm about to learn.

I whip the car into a parking space in the sparsely filled lot and briskly walk to the front door of the restaurant near my house—a restaurant I've been frequenting so often that some of us refer to it as my cafeteria.

I swing the door open and step through the entryway onto the tile floor. In the dim lighting, my eyes sweep the room, looking for Lauren. I spot her almost immediately. She is sitting in a booth at the back of the restaurant near the bar, just as she described.

We have less than an hour to debrief. And whatever is going

on with her, I don't want to rush what she has to tell me. I want to be a good friend. I want to be a great friend. It's important that I listen and be here for her.

Lauren is sitting in front of a stack of papers face down on the table next to her nearly finished cocktail. Even with the faint lighting, I can see tears streaming down her face. This is serious. There's something major on her mind.

I conjure up different scenarios in my head.

Is there something wrong with her dad?

Did something happen to her kid?

Is everything okay with her marriage?

An immense amount of possibilities run through my mind.

What could possibly be going on?

Seeing Lauren cry tears of sorrow rather than crying from laughter is another new experience for me. Whatever's going on is massive. She slides out of the booth and stands to greet me with her arms held wide. I walk into her arms, my arms below hers because she has a couple of inches on me, and we embrace in the way you expect close friends to hug during a major crisis—a crisis that I'm eager for her to bring me up to speed on.

Did someone die?

Why wouldn't she give me a glimpse of information about any of these scenarios over the phone?

She orders her second drink—probably her second for the year—and I order a big glass of bold and dry red wine. She orders a vodka soda with a splash of cranberry juice. *Adorable.*

We sit down, and I take my gloves and bulky scarf off to get settled in the booth. Once our drinks arrive, I kick things off by saying with a gentle tone as I reach for her arm across the table, "You have been on my mind all day, and I've been so worried about you. What on earth is going on?"

Lauren trembles and struggles to speak. After taking a few deep breaths, she finally finds the words. She says through quivering lips, "This doesn't have anything to do with me. It has to do with you."

I tilt my head in confusion at this curveball.

She continues, "Well, it actually has everything to do with Chad. I received a call today with a substantial amount of information about him, and I want to know if you want to hear it."

"Yes. Of course I do," I respond with a lump in my throat.

A
CASUAL
ENCOUNTER

(SIXTEEN MONTHS AGO)

Sara's flight had just landed. She was in from out of town to help me celebrate the new home that I had purchased last spring and to spend some quality time together over the weekend. It was Friday afternoon, and I picked her up from the airport.

"Ok, so what are the plans this afternoon?" Sara said as she buckled herself into the car.

"We're going to head out to my brother's and swap my car for his so we can go get the tables and chairs from the party rental place."

My brother James let me use his spare vehicle, a pickup, to get ready for the party.

When we picked up the truck, James asked, "Hey, would you mind if I invite my buddies Mark and Chad to your party?"

"Of course," I said. "The more, the merrier!"

Sara and I picked up the tables and chairs and drove back to my house to set up for the party. As we put up the tables and arranged the chairs, Sara asked, "So who are your brother's friends? Are either of them single?"

"I'm pretty sure Mark has a girlfriend, but I haven't met Chad. So I don't know what his relationship status is. But James has talked about him before and mentioned trying to set us up."

"Why haven't you gone out on a date then?"

"For starters, I don't think it's a good idea to date my brother's friends. Plus, he has kids."

"Oh yes, that definitely adds another layer of complexity."

We noticed the food truck arriving and needed to help give direction as they backed their truck into the driveway. Sara said, "Hold that thought."

As the caterers prepared the food for guests, Brad the bartender pulled in and unloaded his portable bar and the rest of his gear to set up. A few years ago, I discovered the concept of hiring a bartender for my parties. I found that I would spend my entire party making cocktails for people and never get the opportunity to enjoy my guests and my own party. So now, Brad the bartender helps take care of me and my guests.

This party just happened to include roughly forty of my closest friends and new neighbors. It was fun watching everyone line up to the walk-up window of the food truck and the bar where Brad is positioned to make them a signature cocktail or a fun beverage of their choice.

One of my neighbors struck up a conversation with me standing in line. "Welcome to the neighborhood! Where did you move from?"

"Thanks! I was just about fifteen minutes west of here, so not too far."

"Oh that's great. Is this your first home?"

"Well, it's my first single-family home, but I do have two townhomes. I rent them both out," I said as we stepped forward in the line.

"That's fantastic! Good for you. Did you plan to become a landlord?"

"No, it's never something I planned to do. It just happened organically."

"Well, I'm not sure how much history you know about your home, but it used to be a crack house."

"Seriously? Oh wow! It's not every day you hear that. Tell me more."

"It was a revolving door of tenants before they completely remodeled it to make it what it is today. The police even raided it one night! It was quite an ordeal."

"Wow, that sounds like more excitement than I'd be comfortable with in my neighborhood."

"We were so happy to see the makeover on the house and are thrilled to have you here."

"Thank you so much! I'm happy to be here."

Just then, I was pulled away by caterers with questions about where to set up dessert.

I caught a glimpse of James and it appeared as though he might be getting ready to leave soon. I wanted to catch him before he left, so I walked over to where he was chatting with Mark. "What happened to your buddy, Chad?" I asked.

"He said he wasn't feeling well, so he wasn't able to make it," James replied.

"Ahh, well hopefully he feels better. James, would you be willing to take Sara and me out on your boat on Lake Minnetonka tomorrow?"

We were going to his house anyway because I had to return his pickup truck.

He said, "Sure," and asked, "Who's all coming?"

"Just the two of us," I said.

"Oh, I thought it would be a bunch of your girlfriends." I sensed a bit of disappointment in his response.

"No, I wasn't thinking of a party. I thought it would be nice to take Sara out for a mellow cruise and show her around the lake while she's in town."

It was the kind of summer Saturday we live for in Minnesota – where the sun felt like it was wrapping you up in a hug with its warm rays. The refreshing waters of its many lakes serve as an invitation to slip in and cool off.

I glanced across the boat at Sara and watched her quickly slip her sunglasses over her eyes to protect them from the bright rays reflecting off the water.

The boat gently rocked back and forth, still tied up to the dock. I saw Sara grab hold of the side of the boat and let out a deep exhale. Her body language made me wonder if she was also feeling the effects of the copious amounts of wine we imbibed last night.

We sat with James and waited for his friend, Chad, to arrive before we could take off for our cruise around the lake. James hadn't mentioned that he had invited any friends, but it was his boat, and he could certainly invite who he wanted.

James had told me about his friend, Chad. As I mentioned to Sara yesterday, he'd even expressed that he wanted us to meet.

Chad had become his personal trainer, and James had invited me several times to work out with them. I hadn't taken him up on it. They had also become good friends and spent a lot of time together, so I suppose I *was* curious to get to know Chad.

Chad finally arrived and sauntered onto the boat with no sense of urgency, despite the fact that we had been waiting for him to leave the dock. He had on navy floral swim trunks and a light blue v-neck t-shirt.

I made eye contact with Chad for the first time as he slid his sunglasses onto the top of his head, pushing back his thick, brown, longish hair. I noticed his display of confidence with steady eye contact. On that bright day, his eyes sparkled like sunlight dancing across the blue ocean. My eyes have always been one of my most notable features, and in contrast to his ocean blues, mine are lighter like the blue skies. Even though I was not initially attracted to Chad, I was interested to see what he had to offer under that light blue v-neck tee. He was a personal trainer after all.

As the day progressed and the cocktails were flowing—a little hair of the dog—I began to let my guard down a bit, and the banter began. I grew to appreciate Chad's sense of humor and quick wit. Not many people can keep up with me in this department, but he held his own.

This was happening in the background while James showed Sara around the lake. As we cruised the shoreline, James pointed at each of the largest homes and proudly stated that so and so lived there.

We were hungry, so we stopped for some food. With the beautiful weather, the dock was busy, and we had to wait for a dock slip. As a smaller boat came by, James pointed and yelled to them, "Use the spaces down on the end so we can use the docks for the big boats!"

We finally got a dock slip, so Sara and I walked into the bustling restaurant on the lake while the guys tied the boat up. There were no tables available. We put our names down on the list and got a buzzer.

When James and Chad walked in a moment after us, I showed James the buzzer and said, "There's a forty-five-minute wait. We put our names on the waitlist."

Snatching the buzzer from my hand, James walked tall up

to the hostess himself. I sank back into the shadows while he schmoozed the hostess. He told her he knew the owner. He got us seated immediately, walking us past everyone else waiting for their turn.

Proudly, James beamed and motioned for us to follow him to our table. I guess some people believe rules don't apply to them.

We ordered appetizers for the table, and Chad suggested we all share a bottle of wine. "What type of wine does everyone like?" he asked.

James said, "Nothing for me. I'm driving the boat. But you guys go ahead."

"There aren't many wines I've met that I don't like," I said lightheartedly, and we all laughed.

Chad replied with a smirk while perusing the wine list. "Okay, well it sounds like you're pretty easy to please." He selected a bottle of rosé to order from the server when they returned.

I noticed the ease of conversation throughout the meal.

After we wrapped up at the table, Sara and I wandered to the bathroom together—partly because this is what girls do and partly because James doesn't let people use the bathroom on the boat.

"Oh my God, Ginny. He's totally flirting with you!" Sara squealed once we stepped inside the ladies' room.

"No, he's not. We're all just having fun and being playful," I said.

"Ginny. You're *crazy*. He's one thousand percent flirting with you," Sara insisted.

"Sara. You're married, and let's be honest… You have zero game," I said playfully.

We both laughed at this, and as we walked out of the bathroom back to the table, Sara got in the last word. "Well, you might be right about that, but Chad's into you."

CABIN

I DIDN'T GIVE CHAD ANOTHER THOUGHT FOR WEEKS. He went with James on vacation to London, where they met up with James' son while I jetted off for a vacation with my friend, Blair, to Greece for two weeks.

Upon returning home from Athens and the Greek islands of Mykonos and Santorini, I received a text from an unknown number with a Minneapolis 612 area code out of the blue.

The message was about going to James and Karen's cabin for Labor Day weekend. Karen is James' wife. They've been together for over twenty years. However, I was still getting used to navigating a new normal after James came home from a business trip to discover Karen had abruptly packed up what she wanted and moved out of the house several months ago. Although they're separated, they still spend a lot of time together.

Chad's been asking both James and Karen for my number, which Karen happily provided him with even though James refused.

I called Sara immediately. "You're never going to believe this. Chad texted me," I said.

"Of course I believe it! I *told* you he was flirting with you," Sara confidently replied after I told her the text was about going to the cabin.

"What should I do?" I asked.

"You should definitely go! What do you have to lose?"

"Oh, I don't know. A whole weekend together? That could be a disaster."

"Or it could be a lot of fun!"

"I guess you're right. It could be fun."

"I like him, Ginny. I'm so excited that I got to witness the day you two met. Send me updates!"

Over Labor Day weekend, I drove up to my brother's cabin on Gull Lake in Brainerd, Minnesota. This was a typical holiday weekend for our family, weather permitting. I loaded the car up with my bags full of gear for the weekend. My dogs, Emilio and Sadie, came along on the two-hour drive up north.

The weekend would be filled with taking the boat out, taking the jet skis out, having fires in the evening, and playing intense games of euchre with the neighbors. This weekend, Chad would also join the crew, so it would be the four of us; Chad, James, Karen, and me, plus the dogs.

I was hanging out in the living room with Emilio and Sadie when Chad arrived. Sadie was very sweet but also very cautious. She had a tendency to bark at various men and kids, so I was blown away when Chad walked in the door and she didn't make a peep.

She sat on the ottoman in the living room and carefully and slowly reached toward him with her nose to sniff his outstretched hand. I've heard that dogs are good judges of character, and it seemed that her lack of barking was a good sign in this case.

He must be a good guy, I thought. *If Sadie likes him, I'm going to give this guy a chance!*

After everyone got settled, we ventured out for an afternoon on the boat. We were slowly cruising along the coastline when Chad asked no one in particular, "If you had to pick a karaoke song, what would it be?" I love a good conversation starter.

Karen quickly jumped in. "I'd sing TLC's song 'No Scrubs'!" We played it, and she quickly realized this was not her jam as she tripped over the words and the quick pace.

Chad chimed in next. "Mine would be 'Regulate' by Warren G."

This was one of my favorite old-school songs, and I couldn't believe that was what he selected. We played it and sang along together.

This sparked a conversation about what type of music we both liked. We quickly discovered that we both love singer-songwriter artists like Mat Kearney, Jason Mraz, and others along those same lines.

One point, Chad.

As we got ready for bed, I pretended I didn't hear the hushed exchange between Chad and James.

"I didn't bring any underwear. Can I borrow a pair?" Chad quietly asked James.

"Here. I can give you a pair of Karen's lacey thongs!" James replied while laughing. I knew that laugh—the one where he's laughing so hard at himself that his face turns deep red.

"C'mon. I don't wear underwear, and I need something to sleep in."

There are three bedrooms in the cabin; Karen and James'

bedroom, a guest room with a queen-sized bed, and a room with bunk beds. I stayed in the room with the queen-sized bed.

Chad had been asking about sleeping in my room with me—in the same bed. He was persistent, but not in a creepy way. He said it felt childish to sleep in the bunk room.

His sleeping in my bed was the underlying reason for him borrowing the underwear. I gave in, agreeing, but *only* if he gave me a back rub… with no monkey business.

My bed at the cabin was a Sleep Number bed. The remote control on my side of the bed was labeled *Ginny*. As Chad got in on his side of the bed and reached for the remote to adjust his sleep number, he saw that it was labeled *Lucky*. He gave me a sideways glance with a smile. No words needed to be exchanged, but this made for a good chuckle as we settled in on the first evening.

We stayed up until at least two o'clock in the morning talking. Not me as much, but Chad did quite a bit of talking. I had never considered myself a "talker." You wouldn't have found me gushing about my feelings. Talking about myself made me feel uncomfortable, especially with a new person.

He opened up to me and told me about his marriage and past relationships and why they failed.

I asked Chad why he got divorced.

Chad explained, "Elsa and I were like roommates. There was no passion, but we still get along really well. We're great co-parents. In fact, I'd even say we're still close friends."

This seemed like a noble concept, especially because they have children together and they'll be in each other's lives in some capacity forever.

"It's unusual for me to open up and share like this, but you make me feel really comfortable," Chad said.

Although we covered some of these more serious topics, we also got to know silly things about each other, too.

Chad asked me, "What's your favorite candy?"

"Hmmm, I'd probably have to say Sour Patch Kids if I could only pick one," I said.

"Oh my gosh, no way! That's my favorite candy. We're totally getting married!" And we both burst out in laughter.

The following day, Karen and I were in the dining room watching James and Chad make waves on the water with the jet skis. I could sense that Karen wanted to seize the opportunity to get the intel on Chad.

"What do you think? Do you like him?"

I replied, "I'm just not quite sure what to think yet."

I didn't feel a strong pull toward him, nor a strong desire to run in the other direction. However, I was open to exploring and getting to know him better.

As the guys pulled back into the lifts on the jet skis, we began to pack the coolers with beverages and snacks for the boat. James and Chad got the boat ready, and we set out for another afternoon of fun on the water.

We stopped at a pizza place for lunch while out boating, and Chad asked the group, "Can we get the pizza with light cheese?"

"Of course. That's right. Chad tries to avoid cheese," James confirmed.

Chad said, "It gives me sinus problems, which can eventually turn into sinus infections. It's miserable. So I try to limit my cheese intake as much as possible."

You quickly learn little idiosyncrasies when you spend a weekend with someone.

I was trying to figure out why this stood out to me. It felt like a big deal was being made out of Chad and his cheese. Many of us have things we don't eat because they don't agree with us or we don't like them. I tend to take a different approach and discreetly place my order if it has special requests.

Back at the cabin, the four of us sat on the couch watching TV, relaxing after a long day in the sun and fresh air. Chad leaned into me and put his head on my shoulder. I sense he was attempting to make physical contact with me, which I appreciated, but it also felt a little awkward and uncomfortable.

We hadn't as much as held hands or kissed, and this felt almost more intimate than that—and in front of James and Karen at that. My body tensed and turned a bit stiff. He must have sensed this and sat up after a moment.

I was startled awake in the middle of the night by Emilio. He was having one of his episodes that the vet calls optical seizures. He would pant, pace, and cry. It's like he's in pain, and it's not even him inside of his own little body. He tried to hide under things or go into corners. I felt helpless when this happened because there's nothing I could do to help him. We tried different medications over the years, but nothing helped. He didn't sleep during these episodes, which meant neither did I.

Like a mother awakened by her crying child, I jumped up when I heard him crying. I turned to see Chad sleeping next to me, and I was reminded that I was not sleeping alone. I quietly and slowly uncovered myself, slid out of bed to not wake Chad, and tiptoed out to hang with the dogs in the living room. I also woke up with a migraine, which only added to my exhaustion.

Chad woke up before everyone else and came out to the living room where Emilio and Sadie had to sleep in the cabin. Karen only allowed them if they were gated in the living room so it confined where the dog hair was.

"What's going on? How long have you been out here?" he asked sleepily.

"Emilio has these episodes. It's kind of hard to explain. So

I came out here to try to comfort him and to see if I could try to keep him quiet so he doesn't wake everyone up," I explained.

"What kind of episodes?"

"When he was around a year old, he was attacked by a pitbull," I said as I gave Emilio some loving pets to try to keep him calm.

"That sounds terrible."

"It was awful. The pitbull broke free from her chain and lunged straight for his neck and flipped him over on the ground. His ear was bleeding, and the next day he started having these episodes. He's had them periodically ever since."

Chad ushered me back to bed and said, "Oh, poor little guy! And poor you. Go back to bed and get some sleep. I'll hang out with Emilio. I've got this handled."

I was floored. *Who does that?* This was especially surprising from someone I hardly knew and had barely met my dogs. I took him up on it and went back to bed. I fell asleep immediately from complete fatigue.

My heart melted when I woke up for the second time and strolled out to the living room to see Emilio sound asleep, lying next to Chad's leg on the couch while Sadie perched on the couch up by his shoulder. They had bonded. And he did have it handled.

Two points, Chad.

"Good morning," Chad said with a smile.

"Good morning."

"Did you get some sleep?"

"Yes, I feel much better. I can't thank you enough."

"It's my pleasure. We ate breakfast without you, but I made you a plate." Chad pointed to the dining room table.

"Thank you." I saw the covered plate of food. I put my breakfast in the microwave and brewed a cup of coffee. I sat down at the table to eat and looked out over the lake, thinking about how much more enjoyable my last day at the cabin would be now that I was rested.

As we wrapped up our final day on the water, we all helped clean up the boat and brought the coolers and towels inside.

Walking up the slightly sloped yard to the cabin, Karen asked, "What should we do for dinner?"

"Should we go to the golf club? Chad hasn't been there yet."

"Sure, that sounds great." We all got ready to head out for dinner.

The server came by to take our order. Chad took charge, which I loved, and ordered two entrees for us to share. He also selected a bottle of wine that would accompany our dishes nicely.

Karen ordered the salmon and said to our sweet server "And tell the chef to *cook it dead!*"

The server awkwardly replied, "Well, the fish is already dead. So you'd like me to ask them to prepare it well-done for you?"

I noticed that Chad and James split the bill, which made me think, *Is this a date?* I kind of liked that. I couldn't remember the last time a guy bought me dinner in an (even potentially) romantic way.

With full bellies, James drove us back to the cabin after dinner to pack up.

Driving home from the cabin, I had no idea what might transpire, but I reflected that I enjoyed myself.

I was over halfway home when Karen called. "Hello?" I answered.

She jumped right in. "Chad just called me and told me that he likes you. A lot. He asked if I think he should ask you out on a date."

"What did you say?"

"I told him, 'Yes, why not?' He was concerned you might say no. But I told him that he'd never know if he didn't ask. And you just might say yes!"

"Interesting. I wonder if he'll reach out."

"Keep me posted!" Karen chirped with excitement.

ALMA

CHAD WASTED NO TIME ASKING ME OUT for a proper first date. I agreed and even began to get a little excited.

Before our official first date, I was in bed in a hotel room when James called me late at night. There were no niceties. He jumped straight in.

"Ginny, don't go out with Chad," he said, almost in a plea.

"What?" I responded, with a huff of disbelief. "I don't understand. You've been trying to set me up with him, and now that it's happening, you're freaking out," I replied.

"Just trust me. I'm only looking out for you."

We stayed on the phone until after midnight. He just kept repeating himself but didn't provide me with any legitimate reasons he didn't want his little sister dating his buddy.

As we wrapped up the conversation, I reassured him. "I'm a big girl. I got this."

I hung up, still confused because James did a complete 180. I was curious, *why is he now insisting that it's a bad idea?*

I was just about to board my plane home from the Atlanta airport. It was the day before my first date with Chad. I was daydreaming about it when suddenly, I felt my phone buzzing. I looked down and saw a playful text from Chad.

"Hurry home. We have a date to go on!"

I couldn't help but smile and get a little giddy.

Chad had been sending flirty and complimentary texts non-stop, and he said he would pick me up at my house for our first date. It would be a nice change of pace to have someone else driving for the night.

I was a bit nervous, and because I would not be driving, I sipped a glass of champagne to take the edge off. I had butterflies flitting around in my stomach as I looked down and saw Chad's text. I was attempting to add some pigment to the arches of my eyebrows to make them appear like they existed. I sat the pencil down on the countertop and picked up my phone, eager to read his message.

It read, "How big of a U2 fan are you? Any interest in going to the U2 concert tonight?"

"That sounds fun!" I replied.

Even if you're not the world's biggest fan, the opportunity to see such an infamous band like U2 in your lifetime is not something many would turn down. The concert was at the new stadium, which was built the previous year, so it was also a chance for me to check out an exciting new venue.

How do you score last-minute tickets to a U2 concert?

Excited about this turn of events, I gave my makeup its finishing touch and walked to the front of the house to wait for Chad.

I was pacing around in the kitchen in my simple black sweater, jeans and pumps. Anxiously awaiting his arrival, I watched him pull into my driveway. He backed his brown, two-door BMW 3-series coupe into my driveway. It crossed my mind that this is to position the passenger door closer to where my sidewalk meets the driveway from the front door, making it easier for me to get into the car. Thoughtful and sweet, I smiled to myself at the gesture.

For a split second, I recalled Karen telling me a story about a girl he'd recently dated that keyed his car. I guess you could say they didn't end on good terms. I also wondered if he may have backed the car in so I wouldn't see the key marks, but I quickly filed that thought away.

Even though I was expecting it, the sound of the doorbell startled me. I opened the door to see Chad beaming. He held his arm out for me to slip mine into and walked me to his car. I slid into the passenger seat as he opened the car door for me and waited until I was buckled in before shutting the door. I took in how clean and tidy the inside of his car was as he walked around to the driver's side and got in.

Chad informed me that he would be taking me to restaurant Alma, one of the best restaurants in the Twin Cities. Alma is not just a restaurant; it also has a more casual café and a boutique hotel with only a handful of rooms.

One of the things that appealed to me about Chad was that he ran his own business. He was a personal trainer and nutritionist, which demonstrated a certain level of motivation, drive, and dedication to serving his clients.

"Do you mind if I make a quick phone call? I need to call a doctor to discuss a client," Chad asked politely.

It was one of the chiropractors Chad worked with through a local nutrition company.

"Of course, no problem," I said in the most nonchalant, laid-back tone I could. I tried not to be annoyed that he was making a work call less than five minutes into our first date, but it was interesting to sit back and listen to their discussion around their shared client.

Mildly impressed, I thought, *Maybe I've finally met an equal, a partner, someone who also has the ambition to be successful.*

Three points, Chad.

Chad and I approached the host stand at Alma, and he confidently said, "We have a reservation for Chad Silver."

"Oh yes, right this way, Mr. Silver." We were escorted through the restaurant to the bar, where we were seated side by side. He was charming and friendly to the bartender and even struck up a conversation with the older couple sitting next to us.

After Chad paid our bill, he ordered us a rideshare car service to the concert. We arrived at the stadium and made it through security. We proceeded straight to the club level to meet up with Chad's friend, Kevin, who got the concert tickets.

When we entered the club, it didn't take long for Chad to spot Kevin and his friend. We walked over, and he introduced us.

"Kevin, this is Ginny." Chad motioned toward me with a proud smile.

"Hi, it's nice to meet you. I've heard many great things." Kevin said. I noticed a slight hint of an accent when he spoke. There was a stark contrast between my pale flesh and his olive skin as he shook my hand. "Shall we grab cocktails and go to our seats?" he asked. It was more of a statement than a question.

The four of us walked over to the bar, ordered drinks, and sat in our seats just in time for the lights to go down and the concert to begin.

A few songs in, Chad reached down and placed his hand on my shin and calf. He began caressing my leg. As he slid his hand up and down from my ankle to my knee, electricity shot through my body. I turned to look at him, and just then, he leaned over, took my chin between his fingers and thumb, and turned my face toward his to place his lips on mine. Although I was not prepared for it, it was effortless to close my eyes and lean into our first kiss.

As Chad drove me home, I felt a little euphoric. I needed to wrap my head around whether it was from the vodka, the date, or a combination of the two. I appreciated that he didn't ask to come inside. He simply grabbed my face with both hands and gave me a long, slow, passionate kiss on my front doorstep. He pulled away with a smile and said, "I can't wait to see you again."

I said, "Thank you for a great night."

As he walked to his car, I unlocked the front door and walked inside. I stepped inside, turned around, and leaned against the door as it closed. I dropped my hands to my sides. *What just happened? Who IS this guy?*

MOVING
FAST

CHAD PROMPTLY ASKED ME ON A SECOND DATE, requesting to cook dinner for me at his apartment. He was adamant that he wanted to see me before he left for a work trip early Tuesday morning. I let him know that my first availability was Monday.

Although many people might describe me as open and liberal, I tend to err on the conservative side when it comes to dating. My inclination is to take things slow, especially if I like someone.

I was not opposed to going to his apartment for our second date, but I was opposed to spending the night. However, just in case, I packed a bag. I left it discreetly tucked away in the trunk of my car. I didn't want to walk in with an overnight bag and give Chad any ideas.

For dinner, Chad grilled salmon garnished with dill, paired with a side of vegetables. He poured me a glass of sparkling rosé from the bottle that we enjoyed together. I sat at the kitchen table, sipping my beverage as he danced around between the kitchen and the grill on the patio.

As we were enjoying the dinner he made, Chad said, "I have a work trip to Gig Harbor in December. Come with me."

"Where is that?" I asked, stalling a bit so I could process this request.

"It's in Washington, outside of Seattle."

My initial thought was, *Woah… slow down, big guy… This is only our second date.*

Instead, I said gently, "Well, December is a long way away. Let's revisit it as it gets closer."

For dessert, he served key lime yogurt displayed and arranged perfectly with fresh berries, drizzled with lavender honey. It was a work of art and almost too pretty to eat… Almost.

I was taking in my surroundings. We were enjoying a lovely conversation and getting to know one another. Music echoed at the perfect volume on his Sonos system throughout his apartment in the background.

It almost felt like a Michelin-rated restaurant. With all of the attention to detail, I couldn't help but wonder if a straight man could pull all of this together. *Could this guy be gay?* This wasn't a random or isolated thought. After all, he did don skinny jeans and long brown locks. I used the restroom for the first time and noticed he had more skincare and haircare products than you might expect to see in Ru Paul's dressing room.

As I sat back down to join Chad at the table, he asked for the third time, "C'mon… Can't you stay the night?"

"I have my dogs at home," I said innocently. Little did he know, I'd lined up a sitter for the dogs in the event I decided to stay.

I told Chad, "I'm going to step outside to see if I can figure something out for the dogs." I texted the dog sitter to confirm, and I walked out to my car to retrieve my bag that contained my black nightgown and toiletries.

As we were lying in his bed, he texted and canceled all of his clients for the following day so he could stay a little longer with me before he left for the airport in the morning.

He would be in Arizona for a work trip until Saturday. When I woke up next to Chad for the first time in his bed, he said, "You can sleep in as long as you'd like and just let yourself out. Thank you for a great night. I can't wait to see you when I get back!"

Later, I woke up and descended the staircase to discover he had left me a white note with my name in red ink on the envelope. I opened it and inside it read, also in red,

"Ginny—Just wanted to say thank you for giving me some of your time. It's been wonderful getting to know you recently. I mean... —Chad."

This was accompanied by a bottle of the same brand of sparkling rosé we shared the night before. I held the bottle in my hand, debating whether to take it. I felt uncomfortable with him sending me home with a gift after an overnight date. I also worried about leaving it because I didn't want to offend him. *Was this like a $100 bill on the nightstand?*

Although it was tempting, I did not give it up that night. *What would he have left me for that?*

My phone was blowing up throughout the week with flirty messages from Chad. It was hard to imagine that he was doing anything productive at the conference he was attending.

Keeping up with his messages felt like a second job, but his compliments were enough to give anyone a boost in confidence.

We simply couldn't wait to see each other again.

"Why don't I pick you up from the airport?" I messaged him.

"That would be great! I would love that."

"We can place an order for food and pick it up on the way back to your apartment. You'll probably be exhausted after a day of traveling."

I parked my car in the valet at the airport and went inside to wait for him. I stood outside the glass sliding doors by baggage claim and watched passengers shuffling through the airport.

Finally, I saw Chad. I noticed the eggplant colored skinny jeans wrapped around a pair of muscular legs *(an interesting choice.)* He was running his hand through his hair as he walked through the glass doors as they slid apart to enter the baggage claim area. He had a look of pleasant surprise on his face.

"I don't remember the last time I had someone come inside the airport to greet me. What a treat!"

"Of course. Only the best for you," I said playfully.

He caught me up on his travels while we waited for his luggage to arrive. The loud buzzer went off prompting the crowd to move closer. We watched the various versions of black suitcases blend in as they rotated around the belt of the carousel. This made his royal blue hard-sided luggage easy to spot. Walking hand-in-hand, we headed to the parking area where I had parked my car.

Chad asked, "They have valet at the airport?"

"They sure do. I use it all the time. Don't tell anyone. It's one of my best-kept secrets," I said before I pressed my finger to my lips with a smile.

We drove straight to the restaurant to pick up our Italian food and got settled in at his apartment for another enjoyable date together.

Our early dates continued to be food-themed; our next outing was a cooking class. While there were no anaphylactic reactions, it felt like a scene out of the movie *Hitch*.

The interactive environment allowed us to work with each other while conversing and comparing recipe notes and results with others. We stood out as the new, flirty couple, handing each other utensils, sharing in the making of sauces, and brushing up against each other's bodies in passing. We playfully fed each other tastes of our concoctions. This was contrasted by the bickering of other couples. This difference only put us more at ease, thinking that *we'll never be like that.*

After a handful of dates, I determined that it was time to invite Chad over to my place. So I placed an order for dinner for Chad to pick up from a restaurant that's between his apartment and my house. I decided that night that I needed to feel vulnerable and open with him if this thing was going to go anywhere.

Being vulnerable is something that I'd been notoriously horrible at.

We sat down at the dining room table, and I could instantly feel my face heat up in anticipation of what I was about to share with him. It turned red and warm—a natural reaction that happens to me when I'm nervous. I was also uncomfortably sweating bullets, hoping he didn't notice.

"I've been married before," I told Chad. *There, I said it.* It was a marriage that rivaled Britney Spears' Las Vegas marriage in 2004. Okay, it was longer than fifty-five hours. Still, it was one of those situations where I knew immediately that I'd made a mistake.

"It was a long time ago, and it was short-lived," I blurted out.

It was not enjoyable for me to share that, but it was something that needed to be divulged to someone I was considering entering into a relationship with. I felt open, raw, and vulnerable.

Chad gently put his hand on my arm and turned squarely to face me. He softly asked, "That's what you were so nervous about? It's no big deal! I've obviously been married before. And it doesn't matter to me that you were either."

A sense of relief washed over me. I immediately felt comfortable completely letting my guard down with him moving forward.

SOMEONE'S TURNING 40

"I'M SO SORRY THAT I CAN'T spend your birthday with you. I can't get out of this work trip to Nashville," I told Chad, feeling guilty telling him a little white lie. As a rule follower—I stop at an on-ramp when both lights are red, even if there are no other cars—and a terrible liar, this was difficult for me to pull off.

"That's okay, Babe. We'll celebrate together when you get back," Chad said understandingly.

We made plans to have dinner together the evening after his actual birthday when I returned home to celebrate.

Karen, James, Mark, and I pulled together a last-minute surprise party for Chad's 40th birthday. The four of us worked to iron out the details. In addition to the party, I booked us a hotel room at Alma, wanting to tie in something sentimental from our first date.

I landed back in town from Nashville and raced to check in and pick up the keys to the hotel room. Then, I drove back home to take care of my dogs and get ready. I hurried back to the restaurant to get everything set up in the private room where we were throwing his surprise bash.

As it turned out, James accidentally slipped in a group message about the party, so it wasn't truly a surprise for Chad. However, based on the look on his face as he walked through the door, he was surprised to see me.

Over the course of the evening, I was introduced to one of his sisters and her son, as well as his best friend that he had known since they were three years old. We were continuing to let each other into our lives.

Mark had gone by his apartment earlier in the day to pack an overnight bag for Chad so that he'd have clothes to wear to work the next day. I gave Mark instructions through text to try to cover all of the bases. According to Chad, he missed a few items, so he sent Mark back to his place to grab some things and meet us back at Alma.

I wore carefully selected, magnificent lingerie under my dress. I hoped to wow Chad and make it a memorable birthday. I even set out to create the ultimate ambiance by playing appropriate mood-setting music on a portable speaker and burning a candle for a finishing touch.

As things were heating up between me and Chad—clothes were coming off and strewn across the floor—he sweetly asked, "Are you sure you're ready?" He knew that I had wanted to take things slow, and I appreciated him being respectful of that. I wanted to make our first time special and memorable. Waiting for his birthday felt right.

In response, I simply gave him a smile and nodded, and we began to give each other all of ourselves.

As I drove Chad home in the morning, both still high off oxytocin, he turned his whole body towards me in the car and said, "I am so excited for you to meet Taylor and Logan." He wanted to introduce me to his children.

I was taken aback by this. Kids have historically not been my jam. I mean, I like them and appreciate them—for short periods of time. And then I love to give them back to their parents.

This was one of the main reasons I hadn't been interested in meeting Chad in the first place, dammit!

Because I was supposed to be out of town for his birthday, we had plans again that night for dinner. So, I thoughtfully asked, "Can we talk more about this tonight over dinner?"

"Of course," Chad replied.

Over dinner, I waited for precisely the right moment to follow up on the conversation from this morning. It felt paramount to have a more structured and involved discussion about this topic.

"It seems so fast to me," I said, and I followed up with a question that had been on my mind all day. "What does their mom, Elsa, think about this? I'm not a mom, but I do know for certain that if I were, I would want to know who's hanging around my kids."

Chad said, "We trust each other. There hasn't been a specific conversation about you meeting them in particular, but it isn't necessary."

This surprised me, but I appreciated their mutually respectful relationship, friendship even.

Chad was convincing. So we scheduled a time for me to meet his kids. My next date with Chad would be with him, Taylor, and Logan.

We decided it was best for me to come to his apartment and meet them on their turf.

When I entered Chad's apartment, I was greeted politely. Taylor was a spitting image of Chad, with those same ocean blue eyes, but a little towhead. Logan's adorable gap-toothed smile captured my heart immediately. While I've not met or seen a picture of Elsa yet, I imagined Logan must look more like her, having brown hair and eyes.

They quickly dove into a list of questions they'd prepared to ask me that were written down on note cards. One at a time, they began to fire them off at me, taking turns.

"What's your favorite color?"

"What's your favorite song?"

"Have you ever been married?"

"Do you have kids?"

The interrogation was complete. *Whew, I think I passed.* We were now ready to go to dinner at their favorite neighborhood steakhouse. Before leaving, each of the kids wanted to play a song for me and dance to their carefully selected number. Taylor was up first and did the floss to the music. This was followed by Logan doing a little more of what you might call a freestyle dance to "Turn Down for What."

I gave them both a huge smile and a healthy round of applause for their performances. I acknowledged their bravery. It takes a tremendous amount of courage for kids to dance in front of a complete stranger.

Perhaps they were comfortable with me right away? Could this have been an attempt to impress me?

Either way, I could certainly tell that this would be a memory I would cherish. It felt as though I had now been fully integrated into Chad's life. I anticipated that if I had children, it would be important for them to like who I was dating. Feeling like they had just given me a thumbs up felt like I had been completely brought into the fold.

A
REALLY
GOOD
BOYFRIEND

WE WERE HAVING BREAKFAST at Chad's apartment and were discussing a vacation to Hawaii. James had offered for Chad to come along and use some of his airline miles for his ticket as a belated birthday gift.

Before Chad and I had started dating, James invited me to Hawaii with him and Karen and two other couples. I've never minded being a third or fifth or even seventh wheel. This was a trip to the Big Island of Hawaii, which I'd never visited. I had to admit, the concept of not being the third, fifth, or seventh wheel was appealing. At the same time, I couldn't help but speculate if there would be some level of scrutiny around this new person in my life, particularly because everyone was accustomed to me being solo.

Chad said, "I'm not sure if I should go. I would miss a lot of work, but it sounds like a great trip."

Things were still new and fresh with us, and to go on a trip right now together could be awkward or amazing. "I would like for you to come to Hawaii," I blurted out.

"Ok. That's all I needed to hear. I'm coming to Hawaii," Chad said before sealing the deal with a kiss.

This would be an opportunity to see if this relationship had potential or if we weren't a match after all. Things were going well. Maybe too well. Chad was incredibly attentive, things felt comfortable when we were together, and we always managed to mix in a lot of fun.

I was not used to traveling with other people, but Chad was very go-with-the-flow. We were able to arrange our seats to sit next to each other. God forbid we were apart for a few hours. Even traveling together just felt... effortless.

Chad and I were the first ones up in the morning. The time difference from home to Hawaii was a tough adjustment. Our bedroom was in the casita. We moseyed along the path to the main house and got the coffee brewing for everyone. Then, we sat in the hot tub to watch the sunrise together. Once everyone else woke up, we cooked breakfast for the group before the guys went golfing. Just like after our first sleepover, Chad left me little notes. While in Hawaii, he left them on my nightstand.

That morning the note said, "You're my Favorite." This was a phrase I coined as ours in place of "I love you" because those three little words had historically been difficult for me to utter.

The guys were out golfing, and us girls were back at the house. I perceived that Karen was being quite curt with me, which is atypical behavior. This prompted me to ask if the two of us could go for a walk and catch up. It took her a while to open up during the walk.

Eventually, after a little prying, she said, "Seeing you in a relationship is hard for me. It's different. You've been single for a long time, and I'm used to getting my own time with you."

I appreciated her being so forthright, something she didn't exhibit very often.

"And, the PDA between you and Chad is just *too* much. Not to mention, we can hear *everything* going on in your room," Karen said with a sideways glance.

I could feel the heat rising in my face, knowing that I was turning pink.

Well, that's embarrassing. That's my brother in the next room. Is he more bothered by hearing me or his friend?

"I appreciate you being open and sharing that with me, Karen."

It also stung. I was still getting used to her and James' situation and felt as though I needed to be sensitive to that.

And now I have to be sensitive to my new relationship to make her more comfortable? When do my feelings come into play?

Being the people pleaser that I was, I said, "I'll talk to Chad when the guys get back from golfing. We'll be sure to dial the PDA back."

When the guys came back from golfing, I pulled Chad into our bedroom. His excitement dampened when he realized I wasn't pulling him into the bedroom for what he thought. It was really to have a little chat about toning things down. We were lying on our sides, propped up on our elbows, facing one another. I filled him in on my conversation with Karen.

"She's having a difficult time seeing us together. And the PDA is making her uncomfortable. Let's dial things back a bit when we're around other people."

This conversation led to a deeper dialogue about the two of

us and became a defining moment for our relationship moving forward.

Chad gushed, "I'm a really good boyfriend," with a big grin.

"I bet you are. I'll be the judge of that," I replied with a smirk.

We snuck off to watch the sunset on a nearby public beach. We packed up a picnic basket of snacks, a bottle of wine, and a blanket to sit on. Driving to the beach, a Michael Jackson song came on and prompted Chad to ask me what my favorite Michael Jackson song was.

"Ooh, that's easy. But mine's not one of the typical songs that people pick. It's 'Man in the Mirror.'" I plugged my phone into the vehicle to play my favorite version for him, the James Morrison rendition.

We found a parking space, gathered up our picnic supplies, and walked to find an open stretch on the beach. Chad popped the bottle of bubbles and poured us each a glass. As we sat on the blanket and watched the sun disappear into the water, I leaned into Chad's body as he wrapped his arm around me. *Am I turning into a sappy romantic? I kind of like it.*

After our morning coffee and breakfast routine, the six of us packed up our swimsuits and towels for an excursion to swim with the dolphins in the wild.

On the boat, we all lined up at the edge of the back platform in our snorkeling gear as we anxiously waited for the guides to spot a pod of dolphins and position the boat near them.

My heart was pumping in anticipation of them yelling "Go!" precisely when it was time to jump off the boat and glide into the water. The timing and technique was critical to capitalize on the opportunity to swim as closely as possible with the dolphins.

After a handful of times we took a pause from the exhilaration to have lunch on the boat. Once we finished eating, we had one final swim in the ocean alongside the dolphins.

Underwater, Chad grabbed my hand to get my attention and motioned for me to look below us with his other hand. I looked down and saw that right then, there were two dolphins swimming in unison directly underneath us. We turned to look at each other and smiled through our snorkel gear, while gripping each other's hands a little tighter, acknowledging the special moment.

We climbed back in the boat and dried off after the final swim. Chad said, "Wow, that was one of the coolest things I've ever done."

I agreed with a smile spread across my face. "That was one of the best experiences of my life."

Chad replied, "I'm so glad we got to do that together."

It was the final evening, and it was now just the four of us; James, Karen, Chad, and myself.

We were relaxed from our massages and went to a casual restaurant for dinner before leaving for our redeye flight. Leaving Hawaii late gave us the opportunity for some additional sightseeing and one last dinner on the island.

Sitting at dinner, we were overlooking the water, watching the unbelievably beautiful sunset. The photos we captured were so mesmerizing, they looked surreal. But the pictures looked exactly how the painted sky appeared in person. It was the most impressive sunset I had ever seen, and it was the perfect way to end a nearly perfect first vacation with Chad.

Chad and I were relaxing at his apartment, reminiscing about Hawaii and what a magical trip it was. He said nonchalantly, "That was so nice of James to cover all of the expenses."

Chad and I were still getting our bearings in our relationship. I had no idea how much money he made or his financial situation, but I suspected that he didn't make as much as me, which bore no weight. I also considered that even if he was doing well, which he had continuously given me the impression that he did, he also likely had to pay child support and alimony.

We were nowhere near ready to have these conversations yet. I was happy to take on the financial responsibility for our share of the trip. And I didn't want him to feel bad about not paying.

"Oh, I actually took care of our portion," I replied casually.

"What? Why didn't you say anything?"

"I didn't think it was necessary. Karen kept track of expenses, like groceries, excursions, etcetera. She divided everything up by couple and sent me a bill so I could pay her for our share."

"Thank you, Babe!" He pulled me in with a big embrace.

"It's my pleasure."

CABO

"I'M GOING TO GET YOU your own parking space here," Chad said to me from his couch. His apartment building had a heated underground parking garage. I was used to parking my convertible in my garage, so it was an adjustment parking outside when I stayed at his apartment. Having a space in the heated parking garage was enticing.

He continued, "Especially since you'll be spending a lot of time here in the fall and winter." This made perfect sense, because this would also give me access to the building so I didn't have to rely on him or the kids to let me in each time I arrived. He continued to give me signs that our relationship was progressing.

He followed up with, "Hey, can you come over here? I need your help with something."

As I walked over behind the couch and stood looking over his shoulder at his iPad screen, he showed me a list he was making. It was a list of items he wanted to keep for me at his apartment, like a robe, slippers, and dog bowls. This made me smile.

"I also made some space for you in my closet so that you can keep some clothes here. That way you don't always have to haul everything back and forth each time." I also had my own section in the bathroom cabinet for my toiletries. Things were starting to feel a little more permanent—like we were beginning to take the next step in our relationship.

Lauren and I had a trip planned to Cabo long before I met Chad. I'd had several work trips since I'd been dating Chad, but this would be my first vacation without him.

Because Lauren's not much of a drinker, this trip might be the first time we shared a cocktail together. Although Chad's given me access to his apartment, I hadn't yet given him the key to my home. While Lauren and I were sipping margaritas at the pool, I kept getting email notifications from my security company.

"It's saying there's an error or disconnection with my security system." I described the messages to Lauren.

"Do you think the power went out?" Lauren asked.

"It seems like if that were the case, that would happen once. And I've had that happen before. This seems different."

There were only two people I'd given keys to my house—Karen's one of them.

I messaged her, "Hey, I keep getting these weird messages from my security system. Would you be able to go over and check things out for me?"

"Ugh. It was supposed to be a surprise for you when you came home! Chad coordinated with me to install dimmers on the light switches throughout your house. Act surprised." Chad put them in my kitchen, living room, and primary bedroom and bathroom.

I filled Lauren in and smiled in appreciation of how much

thought and effort he put into this surprise, and it truly was something I was eager to get home to and try out.

Lauren and I landed back home from Cabo and I glimpsed Chad waiting for us at baggage claim. My stride picked up a bit as I walked over to greet him. I was excited to introduce him to Lauren. He met me with a lot of affection, which prompted Lauren to react. "Geez, you two. Get a room!"

"I'm sorry, Lauren. I missed my girlfriend," Chad replied playfully. He had been introducing me to everyone as his girl-friend for quite some time. Because he had already given me access to his place with the parking space and garage door opener, it was time for me to continue letting my guard down and let him in, literally and figuratively.

It was out of the ordinary to have a kid-free Saturday night. They were spending the weekend with Elsa and her family. Chad kept a massage table at work where he performed chiropractic adjustments on some of his clients. He brought the massage table home so he could give me a full-body massage. He carefully draped a sheet on the table and then another over me. I got comfortable on the table as he meandered into the kitchen to warm up a bit of coconut oil.

I was in a complete state of relaxation as he neared the end of the massage. He brought me a robe and said, "Just relax. I'm going to go fill the bathtub for you." While the tub filled, he poured me a big glass of red wine and lit candles to create a soft glow and relaxing environment. He wanted me to fully decompress—tonight was all about me.

After being submerged in the bath for just long enough to finish my wine, I stepped out of the tub and got ready for bed. I ascended the stairs to his bedroom to discover he had already let the dogs out, a chore that's typically part of my nightly routine. I heard him on the phone with the kids. I could sense something was wrong.

As I slipped out of my robe and into the sheets next to him, he covered the phone and whispered, "Their cat died" with a frown on his face. "I didn't want to say anything because I don't want to take away from your relaxing night." They were upset and wanted to call and tell their dad. *That's sweet.*

Miraculously, Chad didn't let this ruin the mood. We had become entirely comfortable with each other's bodies, and intimacy came easily to us. This night in particular was spectacular as our bodies moved together between the sheets. We had an active sex life, but that night was out of this world. Chad said that he wanted to make the night all about me, and did he ever. Over and over again.

The morning began the same way last night ended, naked with our entangled bodies between the sheets. Whatever square inch hadn't been explored the night before got discovered and attended to before breakfast.

Ready to take the day on, I slipped into my robe and slippers and floated downstairs. I was sitting at the kitchen island texting Blair. I told her about the massage and bath. "Girl, he gave me five, count them... FIVE big O's between last night and this morning."

I received her response as Chad handed me the pour-over coffee I'd been watching him make for me with care, which was "Jesus Christ. Where's the ring?! Get knocked up immediately! No brainer with this guy."

I was holding back a chuckle with a grin on my face as I cupped the warm coffee mug between both hands and lifted it to my lips for a sip of fresh, hot coffee. Chad noticed my grin and asked, "What's that look for?" with raised brows.

"Oh, nothing," I said mischievously.

I

WORKOUT

LIKE MANY WOMEN, there have been times when I've struggled with my body image. I have fluctuated with my diet and exercise routine over the years.

Perhaps this self-consciousness roots back to the fact that my parents loved to talk about how fat I was as a baby. I weighed ten pounds, one ounce when I was born. *As if I had anything to do with my birth weight.*

My nickname was also "Roller." Supposedly, this was because I never crawled. I'm told I pointed to what I wanted and proceeded to roll to whatever my endpoint was, whether it was a toy or a person. I went straight from this rolling tactic to walking. Apparently, my fondness for efficiency dates back a while.

I've always enjoyed working out and might be considered athletic by some. We often hear someone say that they need to lose weight before they go to a particular gym or workout class. It's a ridiculous concept. Well, I was in that headspace at this point. It was one of the reasons that I've never taken James up on working out with him at Chad's gym.

I hadn't been feeling my best, strongest, or leanest, and I didn't want to look like an idiot or make a mistake... or fail. Failure is not something I handle well.

James called me on Saturday morning. "Come to Chad's ten o'clock group class." He'd come to terms with Chad and me dating. I was not confident I'd gained his approval, but he stopped trying to talk me out of pursuing the relationship.

I scoffed at the thought. "I can't just show up unannounced!"

Things were still relatively fresh between Chad and me. He explained, "Chad's having a rough morning, and trust me, it will make him very happy if you come to the workout."

This was my first time going to the gym where Chad worked, and I was apprehensive to just show up at my brother's recommendation. But he was right. Chad was thrilled and grinning from ear to ear as I walked through the door with James.

I figured it was pretty safe. Even if he didn't want to be open about the fact that we were dating, I could always be there simply as James' sister. He'd been trying to get me to come with him over the past year or two anyway. I found myself enjoying the workout and the people, and I ended up pleased with my decision to go.

Chad had a solid set of clients; some were successful entrepreneurs, lawyers, business executives, and well-known people within the community. It was impressive to see the caliber of his clientele.

I began training with Chad in a couple of small groups throughout the week, when I wasn't traveling, as well as consistently every Saturday morning. I met many of his clients, some of whom he even considered his friends.

One of them being Lou, who typically never came to Saturday classes. But shortly after Chad and I started dating and he told Lou about me, she simply couldn't handle the anticipation of waiting to meet me and showed up on a Saturday morning knowing I'd be there.

When Lou walked in, she wasn't shy about coming right up to me to introduce herself. "Hi, I'm Lou. It's so nice to meet you! I was so excited to hear that Chad has a new girlfriend and couldn't wait to meet the girl he's been gushing about."

There was no beating around the bush with her—in an entertaining way. She was truly curious.

She asked all of the questions that people wanted to know the answers to but were too afraid to ask. Lou was also never afraid to say what was on her mind or give an honest answer, and she did it in a way that felt very unassuming. It's a true gift!

Lou spent her time volunteering as a mediator and sat on the board of a foundation that raises money for children with cancer and other life-threatening diseases. Her selflessness was admirable.

After trying out several different groups and times, I became particularly fond of Lou, as well as Anne. I'd developed friendships with them, which came naturally as we saw each other three to four times per week. This quickly became a routine that I'd grown to love.

Anne walked in just like any other Friday. "Hi, guys! How's everyone doing today?" she said in a warm and gregarious tone. A friendliness that everyone, including me, was drawn to. Anne was outgoing, but she was also quick-witted with a successful career.

Standing back and taking in how fortunate I'd been to have met Lou and Anne, I thought, *These are my people.* They were two of the kindest people I'd ever met.

Anne, Lou, and I developed a good rhythm during our workouts and kept in touch throughout the week. We'd been spending time together outside of the workouts and truly enjoyed getting to know one other and building friendships. I even met Lou's children and husband as well as Anne's partner.

I was gaining a whole new network and circle of friends of solid people. Lou even came to put the kids to bed one Friday night so that Chad and I could go out on a date. She had an absolute heart of gold.

STEPMOMMING

I FOUND MYSELF SITTING in the pickup line after school to get the kids and spending more and more one-on-one time with them without Chad. While I had never envisioned this for myself, I was growing to love this new aspect of my life. When they were alone with me, they were very inquisitive and asked a lot of questions about me and my relationship with their dad.

After picking them up from school, they hadn't been in the car for more than a few minutes when the questions began.

"Do you think that you and our dad will get married?"

"I've never been to a wedding."

"If you and my dad got married, that would make you our stepmom, right?"

"I've never had a stepmom before."

I'd made it a priority to ensure my relationship with the kids was very open. I stressed this from the beginning, and it helped our bond solidify rapidly.

Looking ahead to the weekend, Chad had to work another

seminar, so I would spend the day with the kids. I started research-ing things to do with them and booked them a kids' session at the Apple store at the mall. This particular one taught kids how to program droids for movies.

I enjoyed sitting back and watching them engage. I partic-ularly loved seeing Taylor helping Logan, being the older sibling. Once the class concluded, I took them to lunch at a restaurant of their choice. They picked a well-known fast-food chain restaurant that specializes in noodle-based dishes, so it was apparent I really adored these kids.

After lunch, they asked, "Ginny, can we go for a ride on the roller coaster?"

"Of course! That sounds like a lot of fun."

We walked up to the ticket counter, and I purchased two tickets for them to go on the roller coaster. As we were approach-ing the ride, Taylor slumped and said, "I don't want to go now."

I was confused. I didn't understand why they suddenly didn't want to go on the ride they had been talking about nonstop.

"What do you mean you don't want to go now? Why the change of heart?" I asked gently.

"We thought you were going to come with us on the ride," Taylor said, looking down.

They wanted *me* to go on the roller coaster with them! *How sweet.* My heart melted a little, and I got myself a ticket. The little nuggets were happy as clams that we took that roller coaster ride together... all three of us.

Then we walked over to the JW Marriott hotel where Chad's seminar was being held. He asked for us to come by and say hello. As we were walking over, I texted Chad to let him know we were making our way to see him. He still hadn't responded when we arrived, and he was nowhere to be found.

Many of the people around knew Taylor and Logan, so we

were warmly welcomed. They all knew exactly who we were and who we were there to see, but no one had any idea where Chad was.

I was texting and calling him—still no response. Twenty-five minutes later, with two impatient and annoyed kids, I decided to leave and head back to Chad's apartment.

Chad messaged, "I'm bummed I missed you guys! I was conducting an interview and it was just bad timing for when you stopped by. I'll see you back at my apartment when I'm done here."

Back at the apartment, I could tell something was bothering Taylor.

Sitting side by side, I bumped Taylor's shoulder and asked, "What's wrong?"

"Nothing," Taylor replied.

I wanted to make sure Taylor knew we were in a safe environment. I said, "Okay, but I want you to know that you can talk to me about anything and ask me anything at all. You know that, right?"

"Yeah, I know."

Although I was missing the vibrant colors and crisp air of my favorite season, autumn, we'd been trying to incorporate activities to make the most of the arctic Minnesota winter.

The four of us piled into Chad's car after ice-skating on a chilly winter afternoon. We agreed to stop at the drive-thru at a Starbucks to get some drinks to warm up. Chad was driving, and I was in the front passenger seat when Taylor asked out of the blue, "What's a virgin?"

I was thinking… *shit shit shit*! These conversations were not my area of expertise.

Chad answered calmly and coolly, "A virgin is someone who has never had sex before."

The kids went to church regularly with their mom and were under the impression that sex doesn't happen outside of marriage and that having sex results in children. I don't have children.

Naturally, in response, Taylor asked, "So, for example, Ginny is a virgin?"

Great, they've connected the dots that I don't have children.

I replied rapidly, "Virgin is also the name of a mobile phone company and could be a type of drink without alcohol. And it's also an airline."

Taylor sat up in the backseat, clutching my headrest and quickly responded, "Are you avoiding the question? Wait... Are you not a virgin?"

I struggled to keep a straight face as I looked out the window on my side of the car to ensure I didn't make eye contact with either of the kids or Chad. If I did, I knew I would burst out laughing.

I was eternally grateful to the barista working the drive-up window for jumping in right then and serving our drinks at exactly that moment, which diverted the conversation onto other topics. I recognized that I was going to need to be on my toes a little more in anticipation of unexpected questions. But I was also thankful for this continued bonding experience.

Habits formed. Logan always sat next to me at the movies or in restaurant booths. We had our seating order in the breakfast nook and at the dining room table at my house. Even in the car, Taylor sat behind me and Logan sat behind Chad. These routines, while very unexpected for me, were comforting.

From the beginning, I strived to approach my role in the kids' lives with a tremendous amount of respect for their mom,

Elsa. That was just my nature, but I also knew that if I were in her position, I'd hope for the same.

It felt like it was time to broach the subject of Elsa and I meeting. I said to Chad, "Do you think Elsa would be interested in meeting? It might be nice for her to know who I am, and I'd love to meet her. I'd definitely want it to be on her terms."

"Sure. That's a great idea, Babe. I'll check with her."

"If she wants to meet one-on-one for a cup of coffee or for a quick meet and greet during a kid exchange, that's cool with me too. I just want whatever will make her feel most comfortable." I had been spending a lot of time with her kids, and she deserved the respect of knowing who was caring for them.

Chad told me after speaking with Elsa, "She wants to meet casually, after school."

"Okay, that works for me. I'll meet her during pick up on Thursday."

As I was picking up Logan from school, which was also Elsa's place of work, she and I got the opportunity to meet. I was nervous. As I pulled up, she was standing outside in the cold in her long black, puffy coat. She was standing behind Logan with her arms draped over Logan's shoulders, almost in a protective stance. I noticed that Logan did indeed resemble Elsa quite a bit.

I got out of my car and walked around to the passenger side to introduce myself.

"Hi Elsa, I'm Ginny," I greeted her with my friendliest tone.

"Hi. I've heard so much about you from the kids." It was easy to tell that she had a warm and gentle soul. She was soft-spoken and almost seemed a little timid. Even though the introduction was brief, I could feel her warmth toward me and, more importantly, toward her children. I was immediately given the impression that they were her number one priority. This didn't intimidate me, but rather made me want to participate in giving these kids the best care possible.

Driving away with Logan in the back seat, I felt a sense of relief to have taken another step of integration into Chad and the kids' lives. I recognized what a big deal meeting the kids' mom was, and I was content with how well it went.

Mondays were typically Elsa's night with the kids, but she had plans that night. Chad had to work, so I hung out with the kids until Elsa could pick them up from Chad's apartment.

The kids and I decided to play The Game of Life. Well, the kids reluctantly agreed to play The Game of Life with me. But they sure were having fun pretending that the pink peg in the passenger seat was me and the blue peg in the driver's seat was Chad.

They added pegs to represent themselves in the car. They giggled every time they added more pegs to represent several more children, depicting the big family they envisioned we might have.

By the time Elsa came to pick the kids up, Chad was home. "Hey, Elsa. Would you like to have a glass of wine with us?"

"Thank you, but no. We've gotta get going. I've got an early morning tomorrow," she declined.

Chad stood up from the couch to get Elsa some supplements from the nutrition company he worked for when he knocked over his glass of red wine, spilling it all over the sofa, rug, and coffee table.

Is he nervous that Elsa and I are in the same room together?

Elsa stepped away from the spill and observed as I swiftly jumped up to clean up Chad's mess, with a knowing look on her face. We exchanged an understanding glance with the realization that this whole scene used to include her.

I began to wonder what it might be like to be in her shoes standing in a room with her own family. *Is her version of their divorce the same as Chad's? How does she perceive this woman playing with and caring for her children – is she happy that I'm there or does it hurt to see? Does she wish she were still the one with Chad or does she have a sense of relief that it isn't?*

All of these questions were swirling around in my head. All I know is that I wanted to show her how much I cared about her kids and show her I'm a good person and that they're in good hands. That's the kind of reassurance I would want.

My weekends consisted of spending time in the movie theaters. Chad and the kids loved movies, which meant I was seeing more movies than I ever had before. I'm not the biggest movie buff. Why? Because I fall asleep during movies. It was much less embarrassing falling asleep during movies at home than it was at the theater.

Chad bought four tickets for us to see *Deadpool 2* in the theater when it came out. I saw the first one and loved it, which frankly surprised me. I'm not into superhero movies. But who doesn't appreciate the hilarious and adorable Ryan Reynolds?

We were waiting for the movie to start, watching the previews. After each preview, Logan said loudly and proudly, "I want to see that!"

Then a terrifying preview played. You could hear a pin drop in the theater. Instead of saying, "I want to see that!" Logan slowly said, "I don't want to see that." You could hear the shift in tone. It was hysterical, and everyone in the theater laughed.

While it was funny, it also exposed that they were probably too young to see the movie that was about to play. I felt like a terrible parent figure. But I blamed this one on Chad because he bought the tickets without any input from me. And, well... They're his kids! We were already there, so right then, it felt like all I could do was slide down in my seat and roll with it. I was still navigating this new part of a parenting role in their lives. I hoped to gently provide my input without stepping on Chad or Elsa's toes.

FIRST
CHRISTMAS

I'M A BIG FAN OF *The 5 Love Languages* by Gary Chapman. The concept of the book is that we show and receive love based on five principles; gifts, quality time, words of affirmation, acts of service, and physical touch. I learned that I show love through giving gifts. The gift doesn't have to be extravagant; it's more about tailoring it to the recipient.

Gifts are an exciting way for me to show that I'm thinking of someone, and spending the time to find the right gift for them fills my cup. On the flip side, I am terrible at receiving gifts. It's something that I'm consistently working on improving.

One of my friends gave me a designer bracelet for a birthday gift. I absolutely loved it! It was gorgeous, and it was so *me*. However, it was such a generous gift that it made me uncomfortable to receive it. Her husband made an excellent point that made me reflect. He explained, "Her love language is giving gifts. Imagine putting yourself in her shoes and how happy it would make you to give someone that gift." It made perfect sense! And I've been able to receive that gift and other gifts much more gracefully.

I was looking forward to spending my first Christmas with Chad and the kids. We planned to celebrate together as a family on Friday, December 23, because I would be leaving for Palm Springs, California, on the morning of the twenty-fourth. I was also celebrating Christmas with my friend, Samantha, for happy hour on the twenty-third. I'm the queen of squeezing it all in.

To coordinate all this, Samantha and I made plans to meet up near Chad's apartment so that I could manage my time effectively. This way, I could get drinks and a snack with her and get "home" to Chad's apartment to celebrate, where they were preparing a huge meat and cheese board for dinner.

When I walked through the door, I was still removing my coat and winter gear when Taylor jumped right in and asked, "So, do you think you're going to be 'Mrs. S?'" My eyes were as big as saucers, and I quickly looked to Chad to gauge his reaction.

The kids had started asking me questions like this in private but never in front of Chad. I always responded with something light and vague to keep an open environment that encouraged them to talk to me and ask me questions.

I was caught off guard. I didn't say a word, hoping that Chad would jump in on this one and take charge. I was also curious as to what he would say.

Without enough time for either of us to reply, the next question was, "So, Dad, have you two been dating about the same amount of time that you and Rebekkah dated?"

Chad clapped back, "Rebekkah and I were just friends. She wanted to date me, but I didn't want to date her. That's why we couldn't be friends anymore." This caused Taylor to withdraw, head down. The topic was quickly dropped, and the conversation was directed back to the night at hand.

After the awkward moment passed, we dug into the meat

and cheese board. I was most looking forward to the gift-opening portion of the night. We were still settling into the relationship, so I purchased a few gifts for each of the kids from me, rather than Chad and I getting them gifts jointly. I selected a few for them individually and a couple that they could share based on their personalities, ages, and interests. We let the kids open theirs first. They gave each gift an "Oh cool" and "I love it" response as they opened each one. *I think I nailed it!* They each had a clear favorite or two.

It was my turn. I was sizing up this rather large box on my lap and was stumped as to what could be inside. I finally got all of the wrapping paper and tape off to discover that Chad got me a set of Sonos speakers. I loved the environment his system created at his apartment and I couldn't wait to have him set them up at my house.

In true form for someone whose love language is gift-giving, I spent significant time thinking about the perfect gift for Chad. Our relationship had proven to be quite special very quickly and I wanted the gift to be reflective of that. I wanted it to feel meaningful. And Chad's apartment, which was lacking in the art department, needed a woman's touch.

Since Alma was a monumental place of firsts for us, I custom ordered a print with the coordinates to Alma on it. I was pleased with how the masculine navy blue inked background contrasted the white numbers and letters. It was custom framed in wood with a metallic accent dripping down the edges. I accompanied the gift with a carefully selected card to celebrate our first Christmas and mentioned that the gift was a representation of firsts for us.

"Wow, this is so cool, Babe. You clearly put a lot of time and thought into this," Chad said warmly.

"Well, my love language is giving gifts," I replied shyly.

Taylor jumped in, "I think Dad's love language is writing notes and giving cards."

Chad and I chuckled at this as he stood up to find the perfect spot for the art. I helped him hang it with the card draping from the wire hanger on the artwork behind it.

Santa came the next morning with one gift for the kids, which Chad had handled. The gift from Santa was a video game, a standard gift for children their age. I was not a parent, but I could appreciate the desire to get them what they wanted. While I didn't want to promote screen time, seeing their joy was heartwarming.

One of the gifts I had purchased was a family membership to the Science Museum. This was such an important gift because it wasn't tangible. Elsa did a wonderful job trying to instill in them that material things and money aren't important. My goal was to align with that message to create continuity and consistency. This experience would be enjoyed together. We were excited to go together as soon as Chad and I returned from Palm Springs.

We enjoyed a quick breakfast and final celebration before they sent me off to the airport.

It was Christmas Day. I arrived in Palm Springs the day before. Chad's flight had just landed, so I jumped in the car and drove to the airport to pick him up while James, Karen, and their friends waited back at the house. These friends were one of the same couples we went to Hawaii with.

Although we'd been in touch all morning, Chad hadn't mentioned anything about not feeling well until I picked him up. He seemed completely fine when I left yesterday morning.

He said, "I think it must have been the hard-boiled eggs I grabbed at the airport in Minneapolis." He didn't look well as he leaned the passenger seat back into an almost horizontal position. *Is that sweat on his brows?*

We arrived back at the house, and he went into my room almost immediately after greeting everyone. After visiting with everyone for a while, I felt like I needed to check on Chad. It was pitch black in the room, and he was drifting in and out of sleep.

I asked, "Can I get you anything? What can I do to make you feel better?"

"Nothing, Babe. I think I just need to rest."

I tried to be a good guest and visit with James, Karen, and their friends, but I felt pulled to keep checking on Chad. I was doing my best to balance taking care of him and making the most of family time for the holiday. Unfortunately, Chad didn't feel well enough to socialize for more than half of his time in California with us.

It was time to take the kids to the Science Museum for a family day. Chad was feeling better, and the kids were excited to see us. When I walked into Chad's apartment, he was sitting at the kitchen island on his laptop.

After greeting each other with a kiss, I asked, "What are you up to?"

"I'm just doing a little after-Christmas shopping. I realized when I was putting away all of the decorations, Taylor and Logan have matching stockings, but we don't. I want to order the matching ones for us so that we all have ones that match for next Christmas."

"Oh, cute. That's pretty optimistic to think we'll be together next Christmas. You know, that's a whole year from now," I said with a smirk.

"Babe! Of course we will!" He laughed and pulled me in tight.

I felt gladdened by his efforts to entwine our lives and build a future together.

NATIONAL
SALES
MEETING

EACH YEAR, MY COMPANY HOLDS a national sales meeting in January, a week-long event, which meant I would be gone Sunday through Friday. This would be the longest that Chad and I would be away from each other since the start of our relationship.

As I was getting settled in my seat on the airplane, I pulled out my notebook to plan the week. I opened the cover, and inside there was a blue Post-it note. "You are adored." I loved how he kept things fresh by leaving me notes and cards to discover.

It was Monday morning. I woke up to a message from Chad saying, "Babe, I hate it that you travel so much. Hurry home."

We acknowledged and made fun of ourselves as being "that couple." We were cheesy. We couldn't get enough of each other. Some of my coworkers came up to me and commented about how I looked different and had a glow about me.

I'd trimmed down a bit and was more visibly fit from my new workout routine. It was becoming apparent that I was in deep.

Chad texted, "I'm in bed and feeling under the weather. I'm not going to be able to work today. I'm just going to stay in bed and get some rest."

I felt terrible for him and would have loved to be back home to comfort him. But, at the same time, I thought, *Again? He was just sick.*

I called him before bed, and he quickly replied through text, "I'm on the phone with Mark. I'll call or text you back before bed."

"Okay. Sounds good." I was a little perturbed at being deprioritized beneath Mark, but hoped everything was okay.

It seemed like Mark took up a lot of Chad's time, even on the phone. They frequently had lunch together and had a lot in common, considering they were in the same industry.

Chad was always telling me about the advice he gave Mark, both personally and professionally. They'd been friends for over a decade. Mark didn't have a mean bone in his body. Some people would say that because Mark is so nice, he can sometimes get taken advantage of. Chad said, "He doesn't have a spine." But even with his criticisms of Mark, I found Chad's patience with him admirable. The amount of time he was willing to invest listening and talking over the phone and in-person was more than most would have the patience for.

I fell asleep, not having heard from Chad, but woke up the next morning to a text from him saying, "Good morning! Sorry, it got too late to call you last night. Mark's a mess. Fill you in when you get back. Hurry home, Baby!"

Because Chad was constantly leaving me notes or cards with compliments, I thought it'd be cute to reciprocate by mailing him a card he would receive while I was away.

Who have I become?

I walked into the business office in the hotel to mail the card when one of my colleagues ran into me in the mailroom.

She asked coyly, eyeing the card in my hand, "What are *you* up to?"

I blushed and said, "I'm mailing Chad a card." *Busted.*

"Oh my God, you are too cute! I've never seen you like this. You are so smitten." She laughed, but in a sweet way.

After a long week, I was thrilled to be home. I kicked off my shoes as I walked in the door to discover Chad had displayed two vases of flowers and a bottle of champagne with a card. Being back together after a week apart called for a celebration.

THE
KID
CAVE

I HAVE ONE RELATIVELY SIMPLE TRAVEL RULE; I don't run in airports.

I ran through the Atlanta airport to catch my connecting flight… in a dress and heels. That's true love—for Chad, Taylor, and Logan.

Chad had an overnight trip for his job with the nutrition company. He needed to stay the night in St. Cloud, a town in Central Minnesota, about an hour northwest of the Twin Cities.

It was Thursday, his scheduled night with the kids, so he needed me to stay with them at his apartment. As was typical, I traveled home from a work trip, hurrying back to care for them that night.

When I landed, I immediately ordered dinner to be delivered so that the food and I would arrive at precisely the same time.

The kids and I had become quite close. They loved their alone time with me, and I loved my time with them. Finding myself snuggled in with them that evening brought me so much joy. *Who would have ever envisioned this?*

I woke them up in the morning and made them breakfast. This was a routine we'd fallen into because Chad had to leave early for work. It came easily, and I enjoyed waking them up and cooking their breakfast before school.

"Thanks for breakfast, Ginny," Logan said politely. Elsa picked them up on her way to work.

As she pulled up in the common area, Taylor asked, "Do we get to have fancy breakfast this weekend?"

"We'll have to see about that. It's a solid maybe," I replied with a wink.

On the weekends, the four of us made a big breakfast of eggs, bacon, fresh berries, and either waffles or pancakes. They called it, "Fancy breakfast, and it was a tradition that we rarely veered from, particularly on Sunday mornings before they went to church with Elsa.

It was the first time the kids came over to my house, and it was just the three of us. They immediately ran downstairs, which I hadn't done anything with yet. It was finished, but it was just an open, empty space. Taylor started planning out how the bedroom down there could look.

Later the same week, the four of us were spending an evening at my house. Taylor said, "Dad, come downstairs. I want to show you something." Taylor brought Chad downstairs and started showing him how the bedroom could lay out. He seemed entertained.

Taylor claimed my lower level and coined it the 'kid cave.'

We all agreed this was catchy and determined that we would call my downstairs the kid cave from here on out.

After dinner, I was doing the dishes and cleaning up in the kitchen. Chad and Logan were sitting on the couch watching TV. I was intrigued to hear Chad's response when I overheard Logan ask Chad, "Dad, why can't we just live here? How much would it cost?"

In anticipation of hearing Chad's response, I slowed and then stopped moving the dish towel around the pot that I was drying, almost as though I was pausing so I could hear better. It's like when you're in the car and need to turn the radio down so you can see where you're going.

Chad replied, "It wouldn't cost us anything because Ginny pays for it."

That seems a little presumptuous. Does he know I'm within earshot? Would he reply the same way if he knew I was?

I continued to make my home a place where Chad, Logan, and Taylor also felt at home. Because we'd started spending more time at my house and less time at his apartment, Chad brought their Playstation 4 over to my place. I never thought I'd have a video game console in my home.

I got them their own beanbag chairs and had a custom piece of furniture made for them. It was a project table that provided them with an area to work on homework, color, play games, or just hang out. This only added to the kid cave and the sense of belonging for the two of them at my house.

I've never been much of a Valentine's Day fan. I'm with the camp who considers it a Hallmark holiday. However, Chad and I still wanted to have a small celebration for our first Valentine's Day together. So we got each other lovely cards. Chad greeted me with beautiful, long-stemmed red roses—and the most hideous pair of leggings I'd ever seen. They were black and white with skulls. I do like skulls; I think that they can create quite beautiful artwork and design. But I'm particular about the type of skull décor or clothing that I like. The issue is that once people hear that I like skulls, they suddenly think of me when they see any random, sometimes even creepy or scary, skull, like these leggings that Chad ordered me from Amazon. To add insult to injury, they were two sizes too big.

I'm not a "size queen." I'm not one of those people that won't buy something because the size they desire to be doesn't fit. But these ugly leggings that were two sizes too big for me were discreetly tucked away in a dark corner of my closet. I'd never wear or speak of them again.

I had spent weeks in advance of Valentine's Day preparing and designing a custom book—a love book. *Have I turned to complete mush?* Each page was customized with characters, images, and text. This took a significant amount of time to compile, and a ton of thought went into it. Taylor and Logan were incorporated into it, as well as Emilio and Sadie.

I was beaming with pride at this gift and was delighted that Chad loved it as much as I'd hoped. He brought the book to work the next day to show it off to his clients, especially those he considers friends. I titled it, *A Few Reasons Why You're My Favorite*.

Chad and I were getting ready to go downstairs and start our plans for the evening. My mind started to drift back to when I purchased my house last spring and how much my life has changed since then.

I had plans to make the downstairs bedroom a cocktail lounge. The bedroom was an oblong room, and being single, I wanted to have a cool space downstairs where my friends and I could congregate.

The layout was planned. I'd change the flooring and create

a seating area and a bar with barstools. I started identifying the furniture pieces I'd purchase to make up my cocktail lounge. As it turned out, plans changed.

After exchanging gifts, Chad and I celebrated our first Valentine's Day by making my "cocktail lounge" a bedroom for Taylor and Logan.

We made a great team. Chad put on some John Mayer in the background as we put together beds and made shelves out of reclaimed wood and black plumbing pieces that formed the brackets. We finished by hanging artwork and making up their beds to surprise them the next day.

We stayed up until nearly midnight getting everything together.

When they saw it for the first time, we captured their reaction on video as they ran down the stairs to see their big surprise. When they opened the door and saw their beds, they jumped on them, displaying pure joy. All four of us felt it.

I stood back in awe at how much they paid attention to the details. I got them each monogrammed bedding and sheets to make it feel special to them. It was clear that they felt a sense of family and home as they asked, "This is for us? This is really our room?"

"Yes. This is your room. Do you like it?" I asked.

"I love it!" Logan exclaimed, sprawling out on the bed.

"Yeah. I love it too! Do we get to stay here tonight?" Taylor asked.

"You sure do," Chad said with a smile.

The kids had never been more excited to go to bed than that night.

SIN
CITY

CHAD SAID, "I'm going to surprise you and take you away some-where for your birthday."

It's going to be Vegas.

I thought this for a couple of reasons. One thing that tipped me off was that he previously mentioned that he wanted to take me there to see the show Absinthe.

I was not the biggest Vegas fan, but I knew I could have fun anywhere with Chad.

I was flying to San Diego for work when he texted me, "I just booked our flights for your birthday trip!"

I opened up my Delta app and SURPRISE... Vegas!

"I have another surprise for your birthday that you'll learn when we get there," Chad told me.

The other surprise was that he invited James and Karen to join us. Karen slipped, so it wasn't truly a surprise, although I didn't let on to Chad that she accidentally ruined it.

We waited at his apartment for our ride to pick us up and bring us to the airport. Our suitcases were packed and ready to go by the front door near the stairs to his bedroom. Chad put his hand on my shoulder and said, "Sit down on the step."

I glanced at him curiously and asked, "Since when did you get so bossy?"

I sat on the step. He got down on his knees, pushed my skirt up to my waist, and reached up to pull my lace thong down, sliding it below my knees.

"Oh my God. Chad. No. We don't have time for this."

"I just need to taste you for one minute." There was no use trying to stop him.

I closed my eyes and leaned my head back while he teased me. Just as I was getting lost in the moment, he stopped. He slid my thong back up my thighs and pulled my skirt back down. I looked at him with my mouth agape as though what he just did was wonderful and cruel all at the same time.

"Our car's here. We have to go. We'll finish this in Vegas," he said as he looked at me intensely. Our passion was undeniable.

At least I know I have something to look forward to in Vegas.

A few minutes after checking into our hotel room, there was a knock on the door. We looked at each other inquisitively, wondering who was there. He looked genuine, while I tried to look authentically curious about who could possibly be at the door. "We didn't order room service," I said slyly.

I walked to the door, and when I opened it, James and Karen were standing there with a bottle of champagne in hand. "Surprise! Happy birthday!"

"Oh wow, thanks, guys!" Hugs were exchanged as they entered the room. It was pretty late, so we decided to save the champagne for the next day and get a good night's rest before a few fun-filled days.

Besides, we could use a little privacy. Chad and I needed to satisfy our insatiable appetites for one another and finish what he started before we left…

SADIE RAE

CHAD AND I BOTH HAD BUSINESS in Salt Lake City, so we made a weekend out of it together. That also happened to be where Blair lived, so this would be an opportunity for them to finally meet.

Blair made a reservation at one of her favorite local restaurants for that night. Chad had worked the convention all day while I conducted my business meetings. Blair picked us up at the hotel, and the three of us went to dinner.

The atmosphere was casual and inviting—the perfect environment for the two of them to get to know one another. We shared some drinks and laughs while they playfully found opportunities to bond over, poking a little fun at me.

That went well, I thought.

The next night, Blair picked me up for a girls' night at her house. I asked, "What did you think of Chad?"

"It's clear you two are so in love! I love that for you. He's handsome, witty, and charming. He matches your sense of humor to a T!"

"Seems almost too good to be true, right?"

"Totally. The only thing I'll say is that… and don't take this the wrong way… if I didn't know you two were banging like bunnies, I might almost think he has a gay vibe. I mean, the hair and the skinny jeans!" We laughed.

Noted.

Karen was holding down the fort back home, watching Emilio and Sadie for the weekend. Chad and I noticed that Sadie seemed to be losing weight, and I thought, *Good for you, girl! Working on that summer body.*

Upon returning home from Utah, I arrived at my place on Sunday evening. I stopped in my tracks, standing in the kitchen doorway. I was looking at Sadie standing on the rug and was in utter shock by how skinny she appeared. It was a tremendous difference in just three days. When Chad got there, he agreed with my observation. We also noticed that she seemed to be breathing heavier than usual.

I called Lauren in the morning to tell her that something was wrong. I said, "Sadie has cancer."

Lauren asked, "What? What did the vet say?"

I replied, "I haven't reached out to the vet yet because I just know in my gut that she's sick, and I don't think I'm ready to hear the news. I'm going to watch her for a few days and see how she's doing."

I may or may not be a bit of a helicopter mom when it comes to my dogs. So as I hovered over her the next few days, I tried to convince myself that maybe she just had a little kennel cough and decided to observe her behavior and health for a few more days to determine if I needed to bring her in.

On Sunday evening, I watched Sadie try to jump up into a

chair and miss. She didn't even get close to getting up. *It's time to bring her in.*

I called first thing Monday morning, and the vet was able to see her right away. I was working from home that day, and Chad was training clients. So I brought Sadie to the vet by myself. I'd been bringing Emilio and Sadie to this vet for almost ten years, and I absolutely loved them, except for how much of my money I've forked over throughout the years.

The vet said, "I'm going to do a chest X-ray first. Then, I'll determine if blood work is needed."

Based on this information, I began to fear that it might be bad news. I was sitting on the hard bench, looking at the empty metal table in the sterile, cold exam room. I'd been watching the secondhand tick by when the vet came back in the room—without Sadie. At this point, I was dreading the worst.

She confirmed my suspicions when she said, "Come on back to look at the x-ray with me. Grab some tissues; it's not good."

I'd never been invited back to this area of the vet clinic before. I followed her past the other exam rooms and the cabinets I imagine were filled with supplies. The staff greeted me with downcast eyes and half-smiles; the look of compassion, or empathy, or pity. I wasn't completely sure. We arrived in the dark room, and she showed me Sadie's X-rays.

She pointed and said, "She's absolutely littered with cancer. I'm so sorry."

The tears began flowing down my face uncontrollably.

There's a lot of truth in the saying "cancer sucks." Cancer was literally sucking the life out of Sadie—my baby girl.

The vet started setting expectations for me. "I'd estimate that Sadie has one week to a month, at best. The cancer is in her lungs so badly that she'll start to suffocate to death. It would be a miserable, painful, slow death for her."

She continued as she handed me pamphlets and business

cards, "I recommend you begin to consider euthanization so she doesn't suffer."

I looked down at the papers in my hand and saw the pamphlet topic was about grieving the loss of your pet. The business cards were referrals for euthanization companies.

No, this can't be real. I was in denial.

I immediately texted Chad the news. I was hopeful that he would want to provide comfort and support. This was a foreign feeling for me; to want comfort from someone—to *need* comfort and support from someone.

Chad was in the middle of a training appointment with a client. So he asked her to grant some grace and end their session early so he could come home and be with Sadie and me. And with no questions asked, she did.

I was sitting on the couch, sobbing, waiting for Chad. I was wondering what was taking so long for him to get home. I realized it was because of the flowers in his hands—two vases of flowers, one for me and one for Sadie—when he walked through the door and came to hold me on the couch.

At thirteen and a half, my girl had lived a damn good life. Still, I was not prepared for this. The tears I cried and the pain I felt were unimaginable. I watched Sadie decline rapidly. She stopped eating. When she turned down filet mignon and bacon, I knew her time was coming to an end.

I started calling the companies from the business cards I got from the vet that come to your home and provide gentle end-of-life care. I would be flying to Seattle for a work dinner on Thursday night. I knew I had Chad's support as he held down the fort at home. He reassured me that he had things covered so I could be away for the night. I ended up taking the redeye home so I could arrive by 5:30 a.m. I was able to get home in time to wake the kids up and feed them breakfast. I got a good glimpse of Sadie while the kids were eating... *It's time.*

I dropped Taylor and Logan off at school and drove to the car wash. I was sitting in the line at the wash when I mustered up the courage to call and schedule the appointment for that afternoon.

This was something that I couldn't put too much thought into. It was a situation where you needed to decide exactly when the moment felt right. I made sure it also worked for Chad's schedule.

I texted him, "It's set. They'll be here this afternoon to put Sadie down."

He asked, "Can we move it to tomorrow afternoon so that all four of us, our family, can be there to say goodbye together? If we do it this afternoon, the kids won't get a chance to have their last moments with her. I'd really like them to be there."

I was hesitant because I felt ready today. Having to make that call once was hard enough, and I couldn't imagine calling back and having that conversation again.

But I agreed. So I called the vet back. They had availability for tomorrow afternoon.

Having that last night with Sadie is something that I'll always be grateful for. I'd never gone through a difficult time or grief while in a relationship before, at least not to this degree. I admit, it was nice having Chad and the kids here to navigate this experience together.

I opened the door to let the vet in when I heard the doorbell. I sensed right away that she was tremendously caring and had a gentle demeanor. The kids, mostly Logan, started asking questions that she answered patiently.

"What's that? Will she feel it? Will it hurt her?" While Logan was asking questions, she multitasked by making clay paw imprints for each of the kids so they would have a memory of her to keep.

Watching Sadie's little body go to sleep in the comfort of

her own bed for the final time was surreal. Even though I knew this was the right thing to do, my heart was breaking. Although Chad had only known Sadie for a short time, he was torn up too. After the process was complete, the vet wrapped Sadie up gently in a plaid blanket and placed her inside a wicker basket.

She asked, "Do either of you want to carry Sadie out to my car?"

Chad immediately spoke up and asked, looking at me, "Would it be alright if I carried her out?"

I said, "Of course," knowing I wouldn't have the strength or courage to do it myself.

As I watched him pick her up and carry her out of the house, I couldn't control the tears running down my face. Chad also had tears streaming down his cheeks. It felt like a demonstration of how much he cared for Sadie. And for me.

The vet came back to the door and said the most precious words to me while handing me a black rock with 'Sadie' written in gold. "I will take care of her as though she's my own until I return her home to you."

SPEED

IT WAS TIME FOR A NEW CAR. However, when your dog that has been by your side for thirteen and a half years dies, it takes the air out of any potential excitement of said new car, even if you're a car person.

Being a car person is one of the things I wish I could change about myself. They're such a waste of money and a costly, depreciating asset. But I just can't help that I like a nice car, and I enjoy speed—as it relates to kinematics, not the drug.

The experience of purchasing this car was quite different from other vehicles in the past. This car was something that Chad and I explored and decided on together. I'd never made a decision on a car with anyone else before. It was always just me. It was the four of us now, and we needed something that made sense. His BMW 3-series coupe wasn't exactly roomy, and I've had a convertible for the past few years, which also wasn't the most practical car for a family of four.

We went to the BMW dealership together to see the best options for us.

"The M550 is the hottest car on the road right now, in my opinion," Chad said.

A sedan, I thought. My last two cars have been convertibles. "I'm open to looking at that."

And then I learned that it has a twin-turbo V8 engine. It was fast.

I'm intrigued.

The sales manager showed us a few models and then broke down the financials. When he shared the monthly payment on the M550, Chad said, "That's not bad."

Meanwhile, I gulped and said, "That's more than the mortgage on my first townhome."

Whew, that's a lot of money for a car.

Chad and I sat side by side in the room as I signed the paperwork. The advisor said my credit score out loud, followed by, "That's excellent, Ms. Priem." This made me squirm in my seat. It felt a little awkward for me to have Chad hear this information. Not for any other reason than that it wasn't something that I'd ever shared with anyone. My finances had always been something that I've kept to myself.

As I handed over my keys to the convertible, it felt like saying goodbye to another part of my old life.

THE

BIG

MOVE

IT WAS A BEAUTIFUL SPRING AFTERNOON. The sun was shining on the blooming flowers and you could see the start of the trees budding and the grass turning green.

I was pulling into a friend's driveway as Chad and I wrapped up a conversation. He was talking to me from his bathtub at his apartment. He takes baths much more frequently than showers, and he takes his bath time seriously. His apartment does have a pretty nice tub. It's roomy and deep, so the allure is understandable.

He was telling me, "I received communication from my apartment building that I need to either sign a new lease or give notice."

I sensed his nervousness on the other end of the line, which was unusual. *That's cute.* I wasn't used to this. Chad typically exuded an air of confidence and authority.

He followed up with, "So, how long should I sign this lease for? Or does it even make sense for me to sign another lease at all? Should we move in together?"

Again, as in most big situations or decisions, my first thought went directly to the kids.

How will they take the news? Will they be excited?

I answered his questions with more questions. "You want to move into my house? What about school? How will they get there? Will they be able to stay in the same school if neither you or Elsa live within the school district?"

Taylor and Logan had been asking about moving into my house, but were we all *really* ready for this big step?

Chad instantly reassured me, "As long as we're both ready for this, all of the logistics will work themselves out."

"Ok then. Yeah. I think we are ready for this kind of permanence in our relationship."

"Alright, I won't renew my lease and I'll start figuring out the details for the move," Chad said.

"Let's figure out a fun way to tell the kids. Don't you think we should tell Elsa first so she doesn't hear it from them?" I asked, wanting to make sure we were being respectful of her.

"I don't think that's necessary."

"Ok, well whatever you think is best there, but I think she should know first. I have to run. I'm so excited. I was not expecting this today. Wow!"

"Me too. You're my favorite. I can't wait to take this next step with you." I could hear Chad smiling on the other end of the phone.

I was giddy and excited as I practically skipped to the front door of my friend's. I was anxious to share the news with everybody. I couldn't help but also be a little nervous about this huge change. I hadn't lived with anyone in nearly a decade, and going from a household of one to a household of four would be a big transition. I wanted it to go smoothly for all of us.

Although it might seem fast to take this step, it felt right. I've never been one to jump into anything, but this made sense. I'm not typically a feeler. I'm a thinker. Maybe it was time for me to start acting on feelings a little more.

I'm stretching myself out of my comfort zone. This is good.

People say that when you know, you know... and that's exactly where Chad and I were at.

We decided to tell the kids together. They couldn't have been more excited. The kids had the entire lower level of the house because we expanded the kid cave. They even had a drum set that Chad got from one of his clients. We picked the drums up, providing the kids with yet another fun surprise to come home to.

We tackled combining households together with zero arguments or fights. We had duplicates of things, like toasters and waffle makers, that we ditched. We both took turns on whose to keep or toss, but we mostly kept my stuff.

Becoming a parent figure was a big surprise for people around me, but it seemed to flow naturally. However, what might surprise some people most is the amount of room I made for Chad in my closet. In a lot of ways, I surprised my family and friends with how I have been transforming my life.

NAPA

I HAD A WORK TRIP TO NAPA, so Chad and I decided to make a weekend out of it. There's something about being in wine country and doing tastings as a couple that has a romantic ring to it.

Traveling together had become natural for us. We got it down to a system. As someone who often travels alone for work, it can sometimes be difficult adding someone else to the equation, especially when you've got the routine down pat.

His overall laid-back demeanor helped keep me calm, even in stressful situations. We didn't have an overly packed or under-scheduled itinerary. It was balanced. We both talked to some friends to get recommendations on some wineries to visit. Based on those recommendations and my previous experience traveling to Napa, I booked our accommodations.

We were both feeling a little under the weather, which made wine tasting a challenge. When you're stuffed up with allergies or a cold, or whatever we had, it makes the actual tasting of the wine a bit difficult. But we gave it a valiant effort.

Driving to our first winery, Chad was in the driver's seat with one hand on the wheel and my hand in the other. He squeezed it, looked over at me, and said, "I can feel your love, Ginny."

"That's good. Because I do. I do love you, Chad."

"I love you, too, Ginny." He squeezed my hand with a little more pressure.

At that moment, our three little words switched from "You're my favorite" to "I love you." I felt a flooding sense of relief. Although I'd known for quite some time that we were indeed in love with each other, I'd been having this trepidation about moving in together without having this confirmation. It seemed silly because they're just three little words—words, not actions—yet I let out a deep sigh of relief as I smiled, looking out the passenger window at the beautiful vines.

Despite our developing emotional intimacy, our physical intimacy this trip was, well, floppy.

This had never happened before, and it was getting under my skin.

Is he not attracted to me anymore? Am I doing something wrong? Am I not enough? Are my boobs too big? What is going on?

My insecurities sank in.

"Babe, I'm so sorry. I don't know what's going on. I want to. I just can't."

We threw in the towel after realizing that it just wasn't happening.

Chad headed home solo to Minneapolis the following day as I stayed in wine country for my meetings.

Back home, I couldn't wait to see Chad as I drove to his gym for my workout with Lou and Anne. I got a text from him, saying, "I need to stop taking Zyrtec. It's affecting my sex life."

He sent this along with a screenshot of the side effects of Zyrtec, which included impotence.

This wouldn't have been that big of a deal to me, but what rubbed me the wrong way was that he said "my" sex life. Sometimes one word can make a substantial difference in a message.

I took a screenshot of his message, crossed out "my" and replaced it with "our," and sent it back to him. It's not like I just lay there!

This took away some of the excitement I had to see him for the first time since I returned from Napa.

Feeling a bit deflated after this exchange, I walked into the gym for my workout.

I hope I can blow off some steam.

FAMILY
TIES

IT WAS A TYPICAL SATURDAY MORNING. We had the kids, and Chad had his ten a.m. group workout. What was out of the ordinary was that we were having a party at my house, *our house*, for Chad's clients. We were full-on living together as a family of four.

Chad wanted to display his new family unit we had formed and let his clients see where he lived. My house wasn't anything to show off, but it was charming and welcoming.

I love entertaining and admit that I wanted everything to be enjoyable for our guests.

Knowing how important Chad's reputation was for him with his clients, I felt there was much to be done to get ready for the party to ensure it was everything Chad wanted it to be. I felt a lot of pressure to make sure it was perfect. I was stressed about getting everything together before the guests arrived, so I stayed back from the workout to get things in order.

There were about fifteen of us, including the kids. Everyone was enjoying the beautiful day outside. Chad refilled people's glasses with champagne while the kids pulled people in one by one to provide tours of the house. They did a thorough job while proudly giving an extended tour of the kid cave.

Chad's clients had a great time, and he was pleased with how the party went.

The following weekend, I took the kids to the community pool. It was a hot day, and it was packed. They were having a blast, so I started to think of other options near home that we might be able to enjoy as a family.

I mentioned to Chad, "What do you think about us joining a golf club for the social amenities?"

It would be great to have a place to belong, especially for Taylor and Logan. Perhaps the kids could meet some other kids their age around our neighborhood.

"That's a great idea, Babe. Let's look into it."

After some research, we chose the club that suited us best and reached out for a tour. It was less than five minutes from home, and the four of us could even ride our bikes there during the summer.

We needed referrals from two other existing members. But because we didn't know anyone who already belonged there, we were required to go on interviews, which we of course aced.

Chad ended the meeting with the club manager by saying, "I can see this becoming a long-term family ritual for us."

And because we live so close, the convenience factor will be nice.

Once the two existing members gave their thumbs up, a credit and background check was required as well. This seemed a little intense for joining a golf club, but they were sticklers about it, so we obliged. I noticed that Chad wasn't volunteering too quickly to offer his banking or credit information, so I filled out the registration with my information, and voila! We were members.

The kids were excited to dress up—to wear something other than sweatpants or pajamas—and head to the club for dinner. Even more so, they loved going to the pool. It was great to see them interact with other kids because that was one of the goals of joining. At their mom's house, they had lots of friends to play with. We were hopeful of creating an environment like that here as well.

The kids and I were waiting for Chad to get home so we could leave. The four of us would be heading to James' cabin for the weekend.

When Chad got home, I pulled him into the bedroom to talk in private. It was important to me that we didn't argue in front of the kids. Plus, it's not like we ever argued.

"I'm feeling really overwhelmed. I just packed everyone's bags except yours. I've done the grocery shopping and have Emilio ready. We are all sitting here waiting for you to leave. It's triggering me because I feel like I'm doing everything. I went from doing laundry for one to doing laundry for four. I went from grocery shopping and cooking for one to grocery shopping and cooking for four. I pay the mortgage and all of the bills. I make sure the lawn gets mowed and the house gets cleaned. I drive a sedan now! All of this is on top of having a demanding job that requires me to travel every week and manage my rental properties. I need you to step up," I say all in one breath. It was the first time I felt like I was losing my shit on Chad.

Rather than allowing me to push him away, he stepped in closer and reached for me in an attempt to calm me down.

"You're right, Babe. I'm sorry. You're definitely doing more than your share. I can do more to help out. Let's go enjoy the weekend and then sit down when we get back and figure out a plan where I can contribute more."

"Thank you." The fact that Chad recognized all that I was doing and that he'd been coming up short and that things needed to change was exactly what I needed. His commitment to chipping in more around the house gave me a sense of relief and helped calm me down. He pulled me in tight to further ease the tension I was feeling toward him, and I looked forward to him following up on his commitment when we returned home.

The kids piled into the backseat with Emilio between them, I jumped in the passenger seat and Chad slid into the driver's seat. Everything's back in order and we're ready to head north to the cabin for the weekend. A ritual that the four of us had gotten into was taking turns picking a song of our choice. Early on, Logan would get frustrated because the only song that came to mind was always "Turn Down for What."

Chad was driving, so I was in charge of executing the music through his phone.

After I clicked play on the next requested song, I opened up the browser on his phone because I needed to look something up. When I opened it, I noticed that the Nicollet Island Inn, a nostalgic Minneapolis hotel, was pulled up. This piqued my interest. I quickly closed it and pretended like I didn't see anything.

Is he planning a surprise? Our anniversary is right around the corner…

I'd become an actual soccer mom, driving myself and the kids around in my sedan after work instead of driving myself to happy hour with my friends. The most unexpected part was that I enjoyed it.

I attended more of the kids' soccer games than Chad because he had clients on Monday and Wednesday evenings. There were several games that I attended alongside Elsa. This was initially a little nerve-wracking for me. At our first joint game, she arrived first, so I walked to the sidelines and said hello.

Do I stand by her, or is that weird? Is it weird if I don't stand by her? Does she even want me to hang out and talk to her, or will that annoy her?

We ended up having a great time. It didn't feel forced, and we chatted comfortably throughout the game.

On the drive home afterward, I was on the phone with one of my girlfriends who calls me M&M. She says that I have a thin outer coating, but once you break through it, I'm really soft and melty on the inside. "M&M, you've got the biggest heart. You just need to let people in to see it," she said.

She celebrated seeing me embrace how I've softened and completely changed my life to include Chad and the kids. On the flip side, she threatened, "Although I love seeing this side of you and how much you've changed your life, I will completely disown you if you show up one day with the soccer mom pin on your jacket or start driving a minivan."

I reassured her that neither of those two things would ever happen.

FIELD TRIP

OUR FIRST BIG FIELD TRIP TOGETHER as a family was upon us. We were going to Huntington Beach, California. The kids had never been to California or seen the ocean before. I set up frequent flyer accounts for them and booked their tickets along with mine and Chad's.

We called this our first field trip because Logan had come to call my work trips "field trips" and often said, "Uggh, I want to go on a field trip!" We thought it was the cutest thing and decided it was finally time for a field trip.

I left on Wednesday. Their fight was scheduled so that the three of them would arrive Thursday evening and we would stay for the weekend together.

We wanted it to be a surprise for Taylor and Logan. They knew they were going somewhere, but they didn't know where. Chad had Mark bring them to the airport and sent me a video of them guessing where they thought they were going.

"Texas!" Logan exclaimed.

Taylor guessed, "Either Florida or California. I really hope it's California. Yeah, California would be awesome. I've never been to the ocean!"

My workday was complete, and I was thrilled to meet them in the hotel room at the end of the day. The four of us walked across the street from the hotel to the beach. The kids could barely contain themselves and wanted to get into the water immediately.

Chad was protective and wanted to go in with each of them so that they could get a feel for the water. Watching both of them see and experience the ocean for the first time made my heart burst at the seams.

As Chad and Logan walked hand in hand for Logan's first time in the ocean, I quickly grabbed my phone and snapped a photo. Capturing those first steps ever into the waves was such a special moment, and I was grateful to have been there for it.

I had been to Los Angeles and Southern California many times. Years ago, I even lived just north of San Diego for about a year. However, I had never done much in the way of tourist activities. We thought the kids would enjoy a Hollywood tour, so we found ourselves on a tour bus driving through the Hollywood Hills. Based on their energy level, this was a highlight for them.

"Look. There's a lambo!"

"Oh my gosh. Look! There's a Ferrari!" they'd say, pointing with excitement.

"Whoa! There's Tony Stark's house!"

We captured some great photos of the kids with surfboards, which they thought were pretty cool. Every time we made our way through the hotel lobby to the elevators, the kids begged us to stop by the oversized red adirondack chair. They loved stopping to sit in it and ham it up for the camera. We created some fun family memories on that trip. I hoped it was as memorable for them as my two big family vacations were for me as a kid.

"That was the best field trip ever," Logan said dreamily, looking out the window in the car on the way home. "I can't wait to go back to the ocean."

I can't wait either, Sweetheart.

I was already thinking about the memories we'd make on our next field trip.

BABY
TALK

LAST SUMMER, I attended a wine tasting at a cute steakhouse restaurant near Lake Minnetonka with Karen and another girl-friend. The owners of the winery were a couple from Minnesota. I loved the wine and the nod to my roots, so I became a member.

This was a wine that I ordered for Chad and I early on in our relationship when we were dining out. He loved it as much as me, so we'd peruse the wine list at every restaurant to see if they had our favorite bottle. We'd probably been averaging a bottle a week of this wine. I was on the winery's mailing list, so I received an invite to an event at a prestigious golf club that they were hosting to announce a new vintage they were debuting. We decided to attend.

As we sat at a table conversing with another couple, they asked if we had kids. Chad responded, "Yes, we have two kids," as he reached for my hand.

I was a little stunned by this gesture. I slowly leaned back in my chair with a smile. This meant the world to me, and it made all of my efforts around trying to be a good partner, parent figure and being integrated into their lives feel validated. Even though I was not their mom, and I would never attempt to be their mom or take her place, I felt like we were continuing to define who we were as a family.

Chad was filling out an order form for wine and said, "I'm going to order one bottle for each year and label them by year for our next six years together."

When the bottles arrived, we did just that together. We got out little white labels and a marker to label each bottle for the upcoming six years that we would drink them, reflecting on our past and visualizing our future together.

"I can't wait to see our life together when we are seventy-five," he said.

I had to correct him. "I'll only be seventy-two. *You'll* be seventy-five. Remember, you're three years older than me."

The following week, we found ourselves back at Alma. We were sitting at the bar, and I was feeling brave and wanted to have a conversation about our future.

I asked Chad, "Where do you see our relationship heading?"

As he turned toward me and grabbed both of my hands in his, he said, "I expect that we'll get married." He said this with a sparkle in his eyes and a smile on his face.

This felt comforting to hear, and a big smile on my face reflected back at him. I didn't have a deep desire to get married, but I would be happy to marry Chad. I wanted to plan our future together. It also felt reassuring to know that we were on the same page.

It seemed appropriate to take this opportunity to approach the possibility of having a baby together. I had baby fever. Bad. I wasn't getting any younger. If a baby was in the future, it needed to be soon.

This made me nervous. Although Chad constantly talked about our future together and growing old with each other, I was uncertain how he would feel about having another baby. After all, he already had Taylor and Logan. It would be starting all over again.

Nervously, I looked down at our entwined hands. "How would you feel about us having a baby? We would make a beautiful baby," I added to help lighten the serious topic.

Chad listened patiently, as he usually did, before he thoughtfully responded. His response made complete sense to me. "A baby would change everything."

Thank you, Captain Obvious. But I also understood what he was saying.

Chad expressed, "I love our family and our dynamic just the way it is, and it makes me nervous to think about making such a drastic change to the wonderful family unit we've created. I'm absolutely open to it, but I would like to ask if we can table the conversation for a few months and revisit it again soon."

While I admittedly felt a little deflated, it also felt fair. So for the time being, we would focus on what we're aligned on; building the framework of a future together.

In terms of marriage and moving forward, the conversations evolved to describing what type of wedding rings we would want.

Chad said, "I think I would want something sleek and modern, like maybe a simple gunmetal band."

We were watching a movie where a woman was wearing a massive wedding ring, and I pointed and said casually, "You can just get me something like that."

He said, "It will be a while," and we laughed it off.

LABOR
DAY

CHAD WAS OUT IN THE GARAGE. So I walked outside on this beautiful summer afternoon to see what he was up to. I found him tinkering with his car.

After the neighbor across the street backed into his car, he decided to finally get those key marks along his driver's side door fixed along with this new damage.

The neighbor was utterly beside herself, but she was relieved when Chad didn't file an insurance claim. She was so grateful and said to me, "He's a keeper. Only good people would do something like that."

Chad also ordered some additional parts. He said, "I feel like my car is starting to look old and worn, so I want to update a few things."

I noticed the pile of replacement parts and asked him, "What are those?"

"A few covers to replace some of the controls on the steering wheel and some of the more worn buttons on the dashboard."

He also ordered a cover for the light on the bottom of the door so that when you open it, the BMW logo displays on the ground. My car had this—a newer model BMW—and I thought it was pretentious, but at least it looked like it belonged on my car. If I knew how, I would have turned this feature off.

When he installed this on his car, it appeared grainy and poor quality, as though he was trying too hard. I couldn't quite pinpoint what I was feeling. Was I embarrassed to ride in his car with this new feature? Was I embarrassed for him? I didn't know what to say, so I just shrugged my shoulders and headed back into the house.

We decided to stay home over Labor Day weekend. I was usually at the cabin every year for the holiday weekend. Each year, the Minnesota State Fair is also held, aka the great Minnesota get-together. I'm not a fan of the fair. It's hot and sweaty and crowded and smelly and full of a bunch of fried foods that I don't want to eat because they make me feel terrible. I attend about once every five years. And I swear, every time I go it's just to remind myself of why I haven't been for five years.

Well, this particular summer I would be going twice. *Does that mean I'm good for ten years?* Chad had ordered us tickets for the Jason Mraz concert. The two of us went for a date night and sat in our seats. They weren't great. It was difficult to see the stage because we were all the way over to one side. And then a few songs in, it started to rain. We didn't have umbrellas, and it was raining hard enough to make it uncomfortable. There were plenty of open seats up in the stands, so we moved up to watch the rest of the show where we were covered from the rain.

Usually music was something that I felt deeply connected to Chad through. But tonight I was feeling disconnected. I looked over and stared at his profile as he was blankly staring at the stage. Even though he was holding my hand, it's as though he was physically there, but his mind was somewhere else.

A couple of nights later, we were back for another concert, this time with the kids. Chad was very excited to announce that he got the four of us tickets to an '80s cover band show. After the first few songs, Logan sprawled out across several seats, sound asleep. That kid could sleep anywhere! Meanwhile, Taylor knew every cover band that got on stage and sang along to many of the tunes.

In the car on the way home, Taylor was still feeling the rush of excitement from the concert. "That was so much fun!"

I turned around and looked at the kids in the backseat. As I swung my head back around, I got a glimpse of Chad in the driver's seat. I took it all in and felt at peace, like all was right in my world.

ITALY

"I CAN'T BELIEVE WE'RE FINALLY GOING!" I said to Chad as I lifted my carry-on bag into the overhead bin. Chad and I were embarking on what I envisioned would be a long, romantic trip to Italy.

We started planning and booking the trip about five months ago. Being slightly type A, I enjoy planning trips. Searching for new hotels, restaurants, sights to see—It's all exciting to me!

A client of Chad's that I worked out with on Saturdays and occasionally saw in passing during the week had visited Italy many times. He and his wife offered up a lot of information, tips, tricks, and recommendations on Italy. In addition, my boss was Italian and had also frequented several different regions in Italy.

We had a lot of help and resources to plan this holiday. Chad's client and his wife were even kind enough to go out to dinner with us one evening to share some of their favorite experiences before we jetted off.

"I can't wait to explore Rome with you," Chad replied. I'd

heard mixed things about the city. But it's one of those cities you have to see for yourself. And we did exactly that.

We ate and drank our way through Rome. In addition to seeing all of the must-see landmarks—the Vatican, the Colosseum, the Trevi Fountain, and the Spanish Steps—we also attempted to visit Rome like a local. We explored some smaller, local restaurants where we enjoyed dynamite pasta and delicious wine. And Chad ate lots of cheese without issue.

After exploring Rome, we took the train to Naples, where a driver was awaiting our arrival to bring us to the Amalfi Coast. As our car pulled up to the hotel in Positano, I could tell immediately that it was incredible. The windy, long car ride was totally worth it. It was luxurious and quaint and romantic and simply lovely.

I learned quickly in Italy that they were still a society that viewed male and female roles in a very traditional sense. Because I made the reservation, the room was under my name. Chad was greeted politely at check-in. "Welcome, Mr. Priem." He continued to be "Mr. Priem" the entire stay. He seemed quite comfortable with it, but we got a chuckle out of it every time.

On the trek from Positano to Capri Island, we had to modify our travel plans. The water was too rough for the ferry to come directly into Positano, so we had to take a car to the next town of Sorrento. On the way to Sorrento, Chad started getting carsick. He was a little carsick on the drive from Naples to Positano, but nothing like this. He started to shut down and become withdrawn, which is a side of him I hadn't seen before. He was feeling so bad that he had to ask the driver to stop the car to get out for some fresh air.

This made me feel anxious inside. We were cutting it close. I was nervous that we were going to miss the ferry.

He knows he gets carsick/seasick. Why didn't he travel with motion sickness medication?

I also felt empathy for Chad and was outwardly doing everything I could to support him.

The ferry ride was brutal. I mean, I was fine. But Chad spent the entire ride over the rough waters in the bathroom. He looked green as he stepped out of the loo when we arrived at Capri Island. We got off the ferry, and he crouched down against the stone wall while I gathered all of our heavy luggage.

We did a little shopping on Capri Island. We were only there for twenty-four hours. We'd heard conflicting reviews from people on whether or not to stay a night here or just visit for the day, but I was glad we opted to stay the night.

I was pleasantly surprised when we discovered an Italian designer, Ermanno Schervino, had a store there. He was a designer that I'd discovered a couple of years ago at a boutique in Palm Springs. I had to go in and check out the shop.

As we walked in, my eye was immediately drawn to the top shelf, in the corner. I spied this gorgeous black and white tweed bag with cognac leather handles and piping. I loved it. I wanted it. But I had to think about it. It was a lot of money, and I was already splurging on this trip!

We had to pass the shop on the way back to our hotel. So I told Chad as we neared the store on our return that I'd like to stop back in there and purchase the bag. He stopped me and said, "I already decided that I'm buying it for you." I was amazed and somewhat uncomfortable but invigorated as he opened the door for me to walk into the boutique. But I couldn't help wondering, *Can he afford this?*

I reminded myself that I needed to be gracious at accepting gifts, and this was a nice and expensive gift. I'd never had a guy buy me a handbag before. I bought these things for myself. It was a foreign yet wonderful experience for me, and I was filled with excitement. I knew the bag would get many compliments, and when it did, I couldn't wait to share that Chad bought it for me in Italy.

When we returned home, several of my friends reached out to ask if we were engaged. It seemed that everyone except for Chad and I thought he would propose on this trip. That didn't happen, but I wasn't disappointed because I had zero expectations. This was something that Chad and I would discuss and plan together. I was finally in a relationship that had open and honest communication. I didn't anticipate being caught off guard by anything, especially a proposal.

SCAR
FACE

I EXAMINED A LUMP FORMING over my right eyebrow as I leaned over the sink, trying to get a better look at it in the mirror. We just returned from Italy, and I was at a hotel in Orlando for a work meeting. I asked one of the healthcare practitioners at the meeting what they thought.

I explained to him, "I noticed it yesterday. It's a little itchy, or almost tingly, and seems to be growing bigger."

He said, "Hmm. It could be a spider bite. Let's see if the gift shop has any hydrocortisone. We'll try that and keep an eye on it for the next day or two."

I grabbed a glass of wine with a colleague at the end of the day and then ordered room service back in my room. I had an early flight home the next morning, and I still had a slight jet lag from Italy.

Chad and I had been consistently communicating, like usual. He messaged me, "The kids made sandwiches for an easy dinner."

"Aww, that's so cute." Everything seemed ordinary.

I was sitting on the edge of the bed when I got Chad's next message. "I'm going to drop the kids off at Elsa's. I don't feel well." This felt like a drastic turn of events.

"Do you have jet lag? I feel a little tired, too."

"I don't think it's jet lag. I feel so awful I just can't even be a dad tonight."

It felt like a wave crashed over me. Something didn't feel right. I just saw him this morning, and he seemed completely normal. He didn't mention having jet lag or feeling off at all since we've been home.

I messaged him again after he told me he was going to bed, saying, "I wish I was there to help make you feel better. What can I do?"

After falling asleep with no response, he greeted me with a chipper message in the morning.

I arrived home to see that Chad seemed to be feeling completely himself again.

That was a quick turnaround from being too sick to be a dad last night to feeling 100% this morning.

Over the weekend, the lesion continued to grow. My forehead and eye area started to swell, and my concern grew along with it.

On Monday evening, Chad and I had a date night. We had dinner at his friend Kevin's restaurant and saw the movie, *A Star is Born*.

At dinner, I said, "I think I need to see a doctor. If this was a spider bite, it should be getting better by now, not worse."

He agreed that it was time for me to see a medical professional.

I was fortunate enough to have a friend who was a dermatologist. She was able and kind enough to squeeze me in first thing the following day.

She walked into the exam room, looked at my face for no more than a few seconds, and told me, "You have early-stage shingles."

"What?" *Isn't shingles for old people? How did I get shingles in my thirties?*

"Yes. You have shingles. You're lucky we caught it early, though. Have you been under a lot of stress lately?" she asked.

"I don't think so. I just got back from this amazing, romantic vacation to Italy with my boyfriend."

This doesn't make sense.

I still couldn't wrap my head around the fact that I had shingles… on my face. Although I did feel fortunate that it was on my face. I could understand how people that get shingles on their bodies may think it's a rash or a bug bite and not seek treatment right away.

To my relief, the medications she prescribed began working quickly, and I was on the mend.

Sadly, that primary lesion above my eyebrow did give me a scar—a friendly reminder of this experience.

LET'S
GET
A
PUPPY

CHAD AND I WOULD BE TRAVELING to Chicago for a few days in early November. Chad had purchased tickets to his favorite comedian several months ago, so we decided to make the most of the trip.

We'd been discussing seeing the musical *Hamilton*—it was in Minneapolis last autumn. Our friends Lou and Anne had both seen it independently and said it was fantastic. I was eager to see the show, and knowing it's been in Chicago for longer, I thought checking out tickets there might be less expensive. Because we were already going to be there, it made sense.

After some research, I found reasonably priced tickets close to the stage. But Chad wanted to buy the tickets because I took care of the hotel and flights. He said that he could get us some decent tickets for even less than the ones I found.

We found our seats at the theater. They were in the balcony near the back of the section, where the gap between the ceiling and seats began to diminish. Unfortunately, the ceiling was so low that it blocked the top portion of the stage. So any time the actors climbed higher in the set, we couldn't see them. Other than that, our seats were great.

I coordinated some business meetings while we were there, and we also wanted to do some Christmas shopping. We took a rideshare service to the outlet mall near the airport.

Looking around, I found a coat I wanted to purchase for myself and a gift I wanted to get for James. The sales associate was less than helpful. I told Chad, "Let's just forget it. They clearly don't want to help. I'm going to put this back, and we can go." I wanted to just walk away.

Chad said, "I know they're not being helpful, but that isn't a good enough reason to walk away from this gift that you were drawn to for James. It's perfect for him." I was grateful because he turned out to be right; it was perfect for James. Besides, my brother wasn't easy to find gifts for.

Before leaving for Chicago, we took Emilio to the vet for a quality of life check. "For being sixteen, deaf, blind, and barely able to walk, he's doing pretty good," the vet said.

After the appointment that afternoon, Chad and I were on the phone. I was looking out the window in my living room. He said, "I understand that you want time after Emilio to not have dogs, but I want to get a puppy together, and I am ready whenever you are."

I'd had dogs my entire adult life. I brought Emilio home when I was twenty-two, and while I wouldn't trade having dogs for the world, it's a tremendous responsibility. Having a dog creates extra work, particularly with a busy travel schedule.

But I had Chad in my life. He was Emilio's caretaker while I was away for work, which made life and traveling much easier. Knowing that he was getting excellent care while I was gone put my mind at ease. I was moved by his support and appreciative of his understanding of what I wanted. This helped move the needle for me toward getting a puppy together.

Chad wanted a Vizsla. I love Emilio & Sadie's breed, but I've always wanted a Cavalier King Charles Spaniel. So we would compromise and get a Cavalier King Charles Spaniel. The vet had given me a contact she thought would be a good fit to find a healthy puppy in this breed. This turned out to be a great referral.

We were connected with a breeder and scheduled a call for when we knew we'd be together and have some downtime in Chicago. We had been on the phone with her for over an hour, being intensely interviewed. I was alright with that.

She explained that she was the type of breeder who was not in the business of selling puppies, which I appreciated. She bred show dogs, and if she had any "left over," she was willing to sell them to the right homes.

It was important to her to ensure that she put her puppies in the best situations, so she took the time to match personalities to the right families. At the end of the phone call, she decided that she liked us, at least enough to invite us for an in-person meeting.

We scheduled a meeting for the Sunday after Thanksgiving. We intentionally planned for a day to meet the breeder so that we wouldn't have the kids. As much as getting this puppy would be a gift for us, it would also be a gift for them. Chad and I wanted it to be a surprise for them, so we had to keep it under wraps.

Even if we did get the puppy by Christmas, which was unlikely, we thought we might tell them at Christmas and make it one of their gifts. We discussed wrapping up a collar, leash, dog toy, or something else that signified adding a puppy to our family.

We envisioned the smiles on their faces, watching them

jump up and down with excitement and hearing a barrage of questions. Because the baby conversation was on hold for a few months, perhaps the puppy would be a good distraction for me.

WEDDING
PLANS

I KNEW IT WOULD BE AN INTENSE WEEK. I was traveling to
Alabama for work, and we had my nephew's wedding in Washington state. Chad met my nephew and his fiancée the previous
December when we took a trip for the nutrition company he
worked for out to the Seattle–Tacoma area.

I've had a special bond with my nephew since he was born.
Chad and I being two of only about thirty people invited meant
the world to me. I'd been looking forward to this for months!

We decided to have a lazy day at home as a family after
Chad's Saturday morning group workout session. Saturdays were
our days with the kids, and usually they were filled with Chad
working in the morning, sports, play dates, and running from
here to there; a lot of chaos.

Chad and I went home after the workout and parked ourselves in the living room for the afternoon—and the evening. I
read a book and colored an adult coloring page. Chad was lying

on the couch having a conversation with my brother on the phone. Then he read some magazines while the kids played video games and entertained themselves downstairs in the kid cave.

I feel so calm and settled today.

As I glanced across the room at Chad, he also appeared calm and settled, which was unusual. I seldom saw him relishing in the moment like that.

Because our scheduled days with the kids were Thursday through Sunday, we would miss our entire week with them. So I asked Elsa if we could trade days to have them on Tuesday. This wasn't our only upcoming trip. We also had a trip booked for our family of four to head to Palm Springs for Christmas. This was a tradition that James, Karen, their kids, and I have had for nearly ten years. Even though Chad came to the desert last Christmas, it would be the first time the kids were included.

Although we didn't have any specific plans to get married, we had continued combining and integrating our lives. Now that we had been living together for nearly six months, it was time to begin discussing bigger life topics, like health insurance, vehicles, and planning for the kids' futures—cars and college funds.

One of the perks I had as part of my job was the company car program. You could either take the company vehicle for a fixed cost or purchase your own vehicle and take an allowance each month. I'd been taking an allowance for the past several years and driving my own car. The company was launching a new company vehicle as part of their program—a GMC Acadia Denali.

Even with the recent enhancements Chad had made to his 3-series, it was approaching ten years old, and he was starting to think about a new car.

We weighed all of our options. We sat down and looked at car payments, insurance, gas, etcetera to determine what made the most sense financially. Then, we went out and test-drove an Acadia. It was nice!

Chad said, "I'm not above driving a $50,000 car."

We agreed that this vehicle was the best option financially and the perfect car for our family. So Chad and I picked out our black-on-black Acadia, and I ordered the company vehicle that would be delivered just before Christmas! Chad would make plans to sell his car. I'd have the Acadia, and he'd drive my M550.

Because I paid for the BMW and the cost of the Acadia would also be coming out of my pay, we needed to figure out how to split the payments. I started exploring the waters with some additional financial conversations. He had taken over a few utilities, but he still didn't contribute to the mortgage.

This prompted me to ask, "What type of retirement plan do you have? I don't know exactly how that works when you're self-employed."

"I don't have one," Chad replied, then quickly added, "I had a life insurance policy, but I had to cash it out to pay for some stuff when I got divorced."

"I've never heard of being able to cash out a life insurance policy. Tell me more about that."

"Well, you can. I did it." He was adamant.

I dropped the conversation. Just because I haven't heard of it doesn't mean it didn't happen. However, it concerned me a bit that he didn't have anything saved for his or the kids' future. I'd already been thinking about big expenses, like college or a car, and saving for them. There was plenty of time for me to save for that.

I can handle it.

PART

TWO

NOVEMBER
PAIN

I'M BECOMING JITTERY as I sit in the restaurant with Lauren on Tuesday, November 13, 2018, and I am filled with angst. My interest is piqued, but I'm also terrified to discover what information she's learned about Chad. Details that she feels are important enough to share with me in person rather than over text or on the phone.

In the booth across from me, Lauren begins.

"Today I received a phone call from a parent whose children go to the same school as mine. At some point, after you and Chad got back from Italy, there was a group of us moms at an event. We were talking about Christmas and spring break, discussing where to go. Someone brought up Italy, and I pulled up your Instagram account and showed them your beautiful pictures."

Lauren explains, "I specifically shared the photos from Rome and Positano, not particularly thinking about who was in them. One of the other parents, Rachel, recognized Chad in the photo. She didn't let on to anything at that time, or at least I didn't notice."

Lauren continues, "It must have been a few weeks ago when I showed your photos of Italy. This morning Rachel called me and shared that she had met Chad at a David Gray concert because her friend Crystal was dating him. She described Crystal as sweet with a heart of gold. She is trusting. Crystal knew that Rachel would be calling me."

She takes a sip of her drink and goes on, "It took Rachel some time to convince Crystal to agree to allow me to share this information with you. She's not ready now but would possibly be willing to talk to you at some point. Crystal is afraid that you will assume that she knew Chad had a girlfriend and she had no idea. Once Rachel got Crystal to agree, she was so compelled to get in touch with me that she looked up my contact information in the school directory. I typed these notes when I was talking to Rachel so I could keep all of the details straight." She picks up the papers and waves them. She takes another drink and sets down her glass.

Lauren picks the papers back up and lets out a deep breath to begin again. "Ok. Crystal said that she has been dating Chad on and off for two and a half years at this point and believed that she was in an exclusive relationship with him. Rachel said that it has been filled with heartache and heartbreak for Crystal."

She looks up at me to check in.

I nod for her to continue.

"Chad and Crystal met on Tinder, a dating app," she explains. "When they first started dating two and a half years ago, he would take her in public and invite her over to his apartment. Crystal described every date as fantastic and over the top. His texts were very flattering and always made her feel like a million bucks. And then Chad completely ghosted her, as she put it. Chad reached out to Crystal and sucked her back in a few months later. They dated again for another six months or so before it ended again. Then in July of 2017, Chad pursued Crystal again, and they dated through the end of the year."

"That's when we started dating," I chime in.

"Yes. Crystal was planning to spend his 40th birthday with him in September and was devastated when he canceled on her because he shared that his friends had made plans for him. After this incident, and considering he had not spent any time with her around the holidays, she broke things off with Chad. Christmas was just too hard for her." Lauren pauses to take a deep breath and sip her drink.

"In the spring, Chad messaged Crystal again, and she told him that she was dating someone, so he backed off until June when he emailed her and was heavily pursuing her again."

"Ok, so he's living with me at this point," I say half as a statement, half as a question.

"Exactly. And then Chad and Crystal became intimate again in August. They had a hotel stay in September and then again on October 11."

"We had just gotten home from Italy. I'm pretty sure I was home with him that night," I reply confidently. My heart skips a beat as I think I'm poking holes in this girl's story.

This is crazy. It can't be true. This has to be some kind of mistake.

"Check your calendar again. I fact-checked what I could, and based on my communication with you, I'm pretty certain you were in Orlando."

I pull up my calendar on my phone.

Holy shit.

"Holy shit. You're right. I was in Orlando."

"How are you doing? Can I continue?" Lauren asks with kindness. I can tell she wants to press on.

I'm starting to feel sick to my stomach. "I'm okay. Keep going."

"Crystal and Chad texted every day for almost two weeks

after that overnight until Rachel reached out to Crystal and asked if they could talk. Crystal agreed, and Rachel called her and told her that Chad has a girlfriend. After the conversation with Rachel, Crystal reached out to Chad. He admitted to having a girlfriend that he lives with. He said that he planned to tell her on their planned overnight date two days later."

I had a work trip that day, I recall. I take a big sip of my wine.

"Crystal started pressuring Chad to talk to you. He told her that he needed time because you would kick him out. Crystal was heartbroken over this news. She was beyond madly in love, according to Rachel. She had to take several days off work. Chad and Crystal have continued to talk, and she has continued to pressure him to tell you about her. He expressed to her what telling you would mean to his life and to his kids. Chad said that things with you are so intertwined that he can't get out. He's trapped."

"He's *trapped?*"

"Yeah, that's laughable," Lauren says with disgust, shaking her head.

"Chad always had an excuse for why Crystal couldn't go to his house. He was in the middle of moving. The house was a mess. He was embarrassed of the mess… Are you ok?" Lauren looks up from her notes to check in.

"I mean, not really. I'm trying to make sense of it all and see if any of this lines up," I say skeptically.

"That makes sense. Can I go on?"

"Yes."

"Throughout the relationship, Crystal constantly asked for affirmations that Chad wasn't dating anyone else, and he provided those affirmations. Chad would often say he's not where he wants to be financially but in the future he'd have more time for Crystal, a house, etcetera. He was still trying to build his business. Based on this, she was confused when she saw his new BMW."

"My car! Oh my gosh. He drives my car while I'm gone and pretends it's *his*? That's gross."

"It seems that way. She says he has made more time for her lately by getting together for coffee during the day. Chad sent her pictures of himself from London, Hawaii, and Italy. He said that he was with clients in London and Hawaii and alone in Italy."

"Well, I wasn't in London with him, and technically my brother is a client. But what guy in his forties goes to Italy by himself?" I ask.

"None do," she replies.

"Rachel said that Chad uses Hotwire to find last-minute deals and that the hotel stays started off fancier, but they've gotten less fancy lately. Chad asked Crystal to pay for the stay in September, claiming he had fraud on his credit card. And recently—she didn't say when—they stayed at Crowne Plaza together."

"He has more credit card fraud than anyone I've ever met in my life." This feels too familiar. I'm beginning to think she might actually be talking about Chad—my Chad.

"They can't stay at Crystal's because she lives with her mom." Lauren explains.

"She lives with her mom? How old is she?" I ask.

"Thirty-six. I asked the same question," Lauren shares.

"Crystal is not connected to Chad on social media. He told her that he only uses it for business and wants to maintain a strictly professional image."

"Well, we know that's not true. He has pictures of the two of us and posts of us with the kids on his Instagram," I explained.

"I know. I told Rachel that. She also said that most of their communication was done through an app. Chad said that it was because he didn't want his kids to get into his phone and see their conversations, much of which was sexting. She did say that they've been texting recently through his phone number." Lauren had written a phone number on a piece of paper. She turns it toward me.

"Is this his phone number?" Lauren asks.

"Yes, that's it," I say. *Well, she knows his phone number.*

"What was fascinating was that even after Crystal found out about you, she admitted to hoping Chad would call and say he was picking her over you. She now realizes the thinking is twisted, and she is starting to heal." She sets the papers down.

I sit quietly, trying to absorb everything. She's floored at my reaction and asks me, "How are you not reacting more? How are you not bawling? It must be because you're in complete shock!"

"This is a lot to process," I admit. "You've had the day to sit with it, and I'm just hearing it for the first time."

"I understand. You're in shock. I was terrified to share this with you because I didn't know how you would react. I was sitting in the chair in my living room waiting to leave to meet you, and all I could think was, 'I am facing the real possibility of losing my best friend tonight.'"

I let out a deep sigh. "Well, that isn't going to happen. It took a lot of courage to do this, and I know you did it with good intentions. You're looking out for me. To be candid, there have been a few situations throughout the relationship that have given me pause, but the only person I've ever shared anything with is Sara. She's been incredibly supportive of the relationship since day one, often claiming responsibility for us getting together. I've never wanted to share any of my doubts with you in case you might form a negative opinion."

Lauren nods to demonstrate understanding. "What do you think you're going to do?"

"I don't know yet. But first I need to talk to him."

The server comes and leaves our bill on the table. They're getting ready to close, so it's time for us to leave.

Lauren says, "I just need to say a couple more things before we go. This is your relationship, not mine. I will not actively seek any information about your relationship. There is no judgment here. I am here to support you in any way you need me to."

She wipes her tears away and finishes with, "I love you and appreciate you more than you know. On my very last day, I hope you're by my side. I'm here for you in whatever capacity you need, and I'll support any decision you make."

This initiates the tears rolling down my face; I feel her love. This is exactly the kind of support I need at that moment from my friend. I'm also facing the reality of the situation waiting for me at home.

As we're walking out of the restaurant, Lauren gives me a huge hug and asks, "What do you want me to do? I can come with you to your house."

"No, that's okay. Thank you, though. The kids are there. Plus, I think I need to handle this with him myself," I say.

"I'll be up all night waiting by the phone. Reach out with any updates." No surprise, she's willing to do whatever I need her to do.

"Thank you. I'll let you know how it goes."

REFLECTING

DRIVING HOME, I'm completely overwhelmed and conflicted. Although I know the way home, I feel lost somehow. It's as though I'm watching someone else's life unfold on a movie screen, but I'm living it. This is my life.

My mind begins to drift back to those moments when I've had doubts about the relationship. I've always assumed that every relationship has its fair share of bumps along the way. I brushed my insecurities aside because I thought when entering into a relationship, doubt was a natural part of the process of getting to know one another.

The first doubt was just a few months into dating. One morning, I was at Chad's apartment by myself after he left for work. I needed some chapstick, so I opened the bedside table drawer on my side of the bed. When I opened the drawer, I stopped and stepped back when I saw that it was full of sex toys.

Chad has never brought up using sex toys with me. I hope Taylor and Logan don't open this drawer!

Naturally, I started to make a mental note and take inventory of what was there. I noticed a theme—the items were in sets of two.

Interesting.

That night, we were staying at my house. While we were lying in bed together, I nervously said, "I don't want you to think that I was snooping, but this morning, when I opened the night-stand drawer on my side of bed, I saw all of your sex toys."

He pulled me close, squeezed me, and said, "I'm so sorry if that was uncomfortable for you. They're mainly from my ex-girlfriend, April. I'll toss them all out, and we can start over together."

He followed up with, "I'm naturally a sexually explorative person. But I've never been with a partner that I've felt comfortable with. Until you," Chad said sweetly.

I was flattered that he had this level of comfort with me and looked forward to uncovering what this would mean for us connecting further in the bedroom.

That's a reasonable explanation. We all have pasts.

There was that day I spent with the kids at the mall, and no one could locate him at the hotel.

Where was he?

Shortly after the mall incident with the kids, I wasn't feeling right in my lady parts. I ended up going to the urgency center because it almost felt like a urinary tract infection, but way worse.

I had a gentleman physician's assistant that took care of me. He was kind and patient with me. I explained that I was in a monogamous relationship, but it was new. I explained my symptoms; urgency, frequency, and a significant amount of pain. He decided to run every test, including STD and pregnancy tests. Everything came back negative. I was almost in tears because I just wanted relief, and without any diagnosis, there was no treatment. So I was left to wait it out.

I called Chad and explained what was going on.

"What can I do? Can I come over and be with you?" he asked.

"Honestly, I kind of just want to be alone," I told him as I curled up in the fetal position in bed.

He said, "Don't worry, Babe. I'm sorry you aren't feeling well, but we will get through this together."

Because it takes a few days to get STD tests back, I asked him to get tested for everything.

"It would be impossible for me to have anything, but I'm happy to go get tested anyway," he assured me.

When my test results came back negative, I sent him a screenshot of the results. Chad replied, "Mine were all negative, too."

Did he even go get tested?

What about those lingerie tags? That felt like a major situation…

I begin thinking about the night in February when I raced home to be with the kids—when I ran through the airport—because he had an overnight work trip. That night, I fed the kids, snuggled them, packed their lunches for school the next day, and tucked them into their beds.

I was wiped out from traveling and was doing my nighttime routine. As I was getting ready for bed, I noticed a tag in the trash can in the bathroom labeled size 36C. 36C I am not. That was not even close to my bra size.

I was flooded with confusion. I reached down into the trashcan to get a good look at it to make sure I was seeing things clearly. There wasn't just one tag, but two. It was a matching panty set, size small.

My heart started pounding. My face was heating up and turning rosy like it does when my body is under duress. I peeked in to check on the kids to make sure they were sound asleep. Then, I laid the tags out on the bathroom counter and snapped a picture that I sent to Chad at exactly 9:30 p.m. with this text:

"These aren't mine. I'm not going to leave your kids alone, but tomorrow morning I'm gone."

And then I waited. And waited. And waited for him to respond. He didn't respond all night. My adrenaline was on overdrive, and I was getting up to pee constantly. My curiosity got the best of me, and I began searching through every cabinet, closet, and nook and cranny in his apartment.

As I was searching through the bathroom drawers, I saw the white top of a prescription bottle. *Hmm. I didn't know Chad took any medication.* I held the orange bottle in my hand to examine the label. It wasn't in his name, and I didn't recognize the generic name of the medicine, so I Googled it. Erectile dysfunction medication. *Interesting.* I opened it to see how many pills were inside—twelve. I filed this information away and continued my hunt.

Once I scoured the main level without finding anything else, I walked up the stairs to his lofted bedroom. I came up empty in the closet and didn't discover anything new in the bedside tables. I got down on my knees to see if there was anything under his bed. I saw four long black straps affixed to the underside of his bed. They had soft cuffs attached to the ends—restraints designed for sexual pleasure.

Chad never mentioned either of these things to me.

After receiving no response from him after over an hour, I texted James, "Can you talk?"

He called immediately. "What's going on?" I only shared about the lingerie tags, and he asked, "Could there be some other reasonable explanation? Could it be a client's? Sometimes he trains clients at the gym in his apartment building. Maybe they needed to change."

"I don't know. I think I'm freaking out so much because he's not responding. I hope it's a simple explanation like that. But I don't think he's trained anyone here lately."

After hanging up with James, I packed up my belongings. After I woke the kids up, fed them, and got them off to school, I loaded my things up in my car. I gathered Emilio and Sadie and left his key and garage door opener on the kitchen counter.

It was mid-morning before I heard from Chad. I ignored him. After he texted me a few more times and didn't get a response, he sent, "Babe, is everything ok?"

Is this guy serious?

"This needs to be a conversation, not a text," I replied.

"Ok. What works for you?"

"I can talk at 5:30 p.m."

"Ok. I have the kids, but I can get a sitter. Where do you want to meet?"

"My house," I replied. I wanted to be on my own turf for this conversation.

"Ok, I'll see you then."

When Chad arrived, he had crocodile tears in his eyes. I was stoic.

What reasonable explanation could there be for lingerie tags to be in his bathroom?

I was willing to hear him out.

We sat down on my couch. I positioned myself as far away

from him as possible, creating not only physical distance, but also an emotional barrier between his heart and mine.

Chad explained, "I don't know whose those are, but they're not mine," attempting to be funny.

I looked at him with a straight face. *Not funny.* I was astounded that he was trying to crack jokes. I was making it pretty clear that I was done with him, that we were over. And his response was trying to make light of the situation one second after he was crying?

After realizing that I'm not messing around, he continued, "They must have been in my overnight bag that I haven't used in ages. I cleaned it out along with some stuff from under the bathroom sink. They came from one of those places. But they're old. You have nothing to worry about."

I looked at him for a second, contemplating whether to buy it or not, before he continued. It didn't sit right with me that he told me not to worry. I didn't appreciate him telling me how I should feel, especially when I was already upset, anxious, and heartbroken.

Chad said, "Look, I have abandonment issues. I think it stems back from my dad leaving when I was three years old."

I couldn't imagine not having the close type of relationship with my dad that I do. It made me feel terrible for him, or anyone, that has been abandoned by a parent. I'm also trying to figure out how this was relevant. "I understand, and I'm very sorry for that. No one should feel like a parent left them behind at three. But how does that relate to this?"

"I'm terrified of you leaving me. We continue to get closer every day. Everything is pointing us in the direction of building our future together. I don't know what this means for us right now, but all I know is that I'm going to fight like hell because I'm not ready to lose you."

There was the time we were startled awake by a BANG BANG BANG BANG BANG. Someone was banging loudly on our bedroom window at midnight. It sounded like they were using the side of their fist.

I shot straight up in bed and gasped. I clutched my chest with one hand as Chad laid there, unfazed.

"Chad, oh my God, what was that? Who was that?"

"Probably just some kids in the neighborhood playing a prank," he said casually.

"Umm, there aren't really any kids in the neighborhood, and don't they usually do ding dong ditch or whatever? Wouldn't they do that at around ten o'clock, not 12:30 in the morning?"

"I'm sure it's fine," Chad said, a little annoyed.

"Well, will you at least get up and go make sure?"

"Ok," he said, slowly rolling out of bed.

"Once you make sure there's no one there, I'll set the security system." I never set the security system because I didn't think we needed it. It always seemed like there was more risk of us setting it off ourselves to let Emilio out in the middle of the night than a break-in.

I'm going to turn on all of the security system notifications tomorrow so I receive them on my phone to put my mind at ease.

Chad came back, crawled in bed behind me, and scooped me up in his arms. "There is no one there. You're safe, Baby. You're with me."

Do I still have that random address that popped up in my parked car updates on my phone?

I'd given Chad permission to drive my car while I was traveling. Because my car was synced to my phone, I got "parked car" updates.

After coming home from a trip, I told Chad, "I got a parked car notification for a location that wasn't your work."

"That's weird. Where?"

I recited the address and said, "I can't tell what type of building it is."

"I don't know where that is, but I never went there. I went from home to work, and that's it."

What's nagging at me the most was that damn October 11 date.

It brings me back to two days after we got back from Italy. I had that work trip to Orlando.

Chad and I were texting a lot, as we always did. We had texted about what was going on that day and the upcoming days as well as logistics with the kids. It was a Thursday night, so it was our night with them.

He texted me, "I'm feeling so horrible that I just can't be a dad tonight. I'm going to drop them off at Elsa's."

The last text I got was around 7:30 p.m., stating "I'm going to bed."

7:30 p.m. seems like a very early bedtime, even if you are sick.

Additionally, because of that crazy incident with the knocking on our bedroom window in the middle of the night, I had the alarm system activated to send me text notifications when doors were opened and closed at home as well as when there was motion in the living room.

There was no motion in the living room from Thursday evening through Friday afternoon—about a six- to seven-hour span.

There was no way to get through my house without the

sensor in the living room getting triggered. Chad was insistent that he was home all afternoon Friday, but there was absolutely no way this was true unless he stood or sat in the kitchen the entire time, which he'd never do. This was completely unfeasible because it was a galley kitchen.

When I asked him about it, he said, "I can't be held account-able for the security system not working properly."

"So, the security system worked fine Thursday and Saturday, but for some reason, during this particular time frame, it wasn't working?"

"I guess so because, like I told you, I was here," Chad said adamantly.

When we returned home from Italy, before I left for Orlando, I counted two erectile dysfunction medication pills in his nightstand drawer. Upon returning home, the pack of two was empty. Clearly I hadn't had sex with him from Orlando. I panicked. I needed to confront him, but I was ashamed that I counted his pills.

I left for the grocery store to call Sara.

She was on the phone with her father. I waited for her call back as I sat in my car in the corner of the grocery store's parking lot. My mind was racing as I tried to wrap my head around all of this.

I'd just taken this man on a romantic trip to Italy for ten days where I paid for nearly everything; both of our airfare, including upgrading us to Delta One. I booked us in luxury hotels. And I even splurged for dinner at a Michelin-starred restaurant in Positano. To be fair, he did pay for one night at a hotel and some meals.

When Sara called back, I was practically hyperventilating. I couldn't get the words out. I was crying so violently I could barely breathe.

"Ginny, what is going on? Are you okay?" Sara asked calmly. I could hear the concern in her voice. "Talk to me. You're scaring me."

Finally, I was able to get the words out between breaths.

"Sara, I know it in my soul. I can feel it in my bones! He definitely cheated on me."

Sara was adamant, "I just cannot fathom him doing that to you. Ginny, there's no way that he cheated on you. There has to be some other explanation. He would never do that. He moved his children into your house. He wouldn't do that to his children. Only a psychopath would do that! You have to go home and talk to him."

I took Sara's advice and drove home to discuss things with him. Before I walked into the house, I grabbed his overnight duffle bag out of the trunk of his car. Exhibit A.

I told Chad that we needed to talk and to meet me in our bedroom. If he noticed that I had his duffle bag in my hand, he did a good job of concealing it as I walked past him. I sat on the loveseat situated at the end of the bed, and he sat facing me on the ottoman.

He was relatively patient and calm when I asked him about the pills.

He said, "I have no idea how many pills were in my night-stand drawer or in that overnight duffel bag. I haven't used that bag since before we left for Italy."

"Okay, then help me understand where they went."

"I don't know. But I didn't take them." I sensed a slightly stern tone.

"I find it strange that you take erectile dysfunction medication in general, and we've been together for almost a year and a half now and you've never talked to me about it. As your partner, it seems like something you would at least mention."

"It never crossed my mind to talk to you about it or not talk to you about it."

"How long have you been taking them? Since before me?"

"Yes, I've been taking them for a few years. Intimacy is important to me, and I don't ever want it to not be able to happen."

"Like in Napa?" I snuck in a little jab.

This wasn't adding up to me. The pills, the overnight bag in the trunk of his car, the security system, the dropping the kids off, and the last message at 7:30 p.m. I pressed on.

"So, you've never cheated on me?"

"No," he said while staring directly into my eyes.

"Did you ever cheat on Elsa?"

"No." A moment slipped by. "Well, technically, I guess yes. We were separated when I started dating my ex-girlfriend, April," he said, still locking eyes with me.

At one point, Taylor came back into the bedroom as we were talking, and I had to imagine that it was heavy with intensity in the room.

Chad said, "We're talking right now and need a few minutes in private." They were planning on going to a movie together, so it was a status check.

We talked for about thirty minutes before Chad finally said, in an even more severe tone—a tone I'd never heard him use before, certainly not with me—"I'll tell you what happened to the two pills. But I'm so pissed off that I even have to tell you this because it's none of your fucking business."

I was more curious than ever. "Okay, great! Well, tell me then."

"Mark went out of town to Arizona with his girlfriend this weekend and asked me to borrow a couple. They were going for two nights, so he asked for two pills. He's borrowed them from me before. Your brother has borrowed them from me, and so has Kevin. You're welcome to call Mark right now and ask him."

He knew full well that I would never in a million years call Mark and say, "Hey, did you by chance borrow two erectile dysfunction medication pills from Chad?" Not going to happen.

And why wouldn't he give them to him in the foil pack rather than take them out of it?

Chad's irritation grew over this dialogue. This was made clear not only by his harsh tone but by his sharp words.

It felt like he was attempting to turn the tables on me when he said, "Had I known there were any trust issues in our relationship, I would have never uprooted my kids and moved them in here. We changed everything," he spat with venom and stood up. I felt invisible as he walked past me out of the room.

THE
TALK

IT'S AROUND 11:30 PM by the time I get home to address Chad after receiving this information from Lauren. I pull into the garage and turn the car off. I sit looking at my unsteady hands on the steering wheel for a moment while I come back to reality and shake my head to clear my thoughts.

I'm so focused on the conversation ahead that I go straight into the house, leaving my suitcase in the trunk. I quietly enter the house to not wake the kids, skipping my original plan to kiss their faces.

Trembling, I walk down the hallway, past the office, the laundry room, and finally the guest room before arriving at the doorway of our bedroom. The hallway feels longer than I remember.

I take one big inhale as I pause at the door for a moment. I exhale as I turn the knob in my hand to the right, considering I want to be careful about how I approach the conversation. I decide I'm not going to give him too much information so I can gauge how he responds.

Don't underreact and don't overreact, I tell myself.

I flip the light switch, and the lights turn on high—no need to use those dimmers he installed—and say, "I suggest you put some clothes on. We need to talk."

It's the strangest thing… He already has clothes on. A black v-neck tee and gray joggers. He has *pants* on? Chad sleeps naked. He *never* sleeps in pants.

Does he anticipate something? Is he prepared?

I'm perplexed. He covers his eyes with his forearm from the light and asks, "How was Lauren?"

"Lauren's fine. She didn't need to talk about herself. She needed to talk to me about you."

"What do you mean?"

I sit down in the chair in the bedroom as Chad sits up in bed. I realize now is not the time to dance around anything. I need to be direct.

"She's connected to Crystal Becker, and apparently so are you. What do you have to say about that?"

He clears his throat and says, "I do know her. We went out a few times a couple of years ago. Then we reconnected and went out again a couple of times right before I met you." He shrugs, brushing it off.

I continue looking at him, but I don't say a thing. I wait in silence, arms crossed, trying to eliminate any sort of expression on my face. I'm curious to see what I can coax out of him without giving too many details away.

He goes on to say, "The only thing that I ever did wrong to her was that I didn't want to see her anymore because she was, well, a little fucking crazy." Maybe she is a little fucking crazy, but I'll figure that out for myself.

A few verbal exchanges and moments of silence pass before I ask him, "Can I see your phone?"

He begins to hand it to me but then pauses and pulls it back, saying, "You know what? No. If I let you look at my phone now, what does that mean for the future of our relationship?"

Little does he know that I'd already combed through his phone. I was never able to find anything. Another insecure behavior I'm not proud of.

We talk in circles and don't make much progress. After about forty-five minutes, Chad asks me, "Do you believe it?"

The only words I can come up with are, "I don't want to believe it."

He shakes his head, scoffs, and violently flings the covers off of himself. He stands up from the bed and stomps past me out of the bedroom into the living room. "I'm going to let Emilio outside."

I scurry after him out to the front of the house, astonished that he's walking away from this eminently important conversation. I mean, we're looking at the future of our relationship—or the end.

Does this mean nothing to him? What can be more important than this right now?

We're now in the living room, he's standing near the front door and I'm leaning into an archway near the back.

He motions between the two of us and says, "I know *this* is more important, but I need to get up in four hours for work. I need to get some sleep."

He gets a blanket and a pillow out of the linen closet and makes himself a bed on the couch. Chad's actions indicate this conversation is over for him. I hear his message loud and clear. I walk back to my bedroom, knowing I won't be getting a wink of sleep tonight.

THE
MORNING
AFTER—
NOT THE
PILL

I HEAR A BUZZ FROM MY PHONE as it dances across the night-stand and look to see that Chad texted me, from the living room, "I'm going to take the kids to school so you can sleep in." *He can't face me.*

This morning's plan is for me to get the kids up and to school. I'm insanely frustrated by his message because that was the whole intent of my request to have them on an irregular night outside of the custody agreement—so I could spend the morning with them and not go two weeks without seeing them. I can't go out there now and let them see me in this condition. I know that there's too much tension between me and Chad and I don't want to put them in that environment. So I stay put.

Because I haven't slept a wink, and even though it's still dark outside, I'm wide awake. I didn't necessarily wake up because I slept exactly zero minutes last night. I can hear Chad waking the kids up and trying to keep them quiet while they leave unnecessarily early. I'd later learn that he took them out to breakfast before dropping them off at school. Chad cancels all of his Wednesday clients.

After I hear the garage door close, I know the coast is clear. I begin to sit up in bed and wonder what he might be telling them. *Will I ever see the kids again? Is Chad ripping them away from me and out of my life?*

My mind, heart, and adrenaline have been pumping on overdrive all night long into this morning. It feels like I've been getting up every few minutes to pee. My entire body, from head to toe, has been vacillating between shivering and sweating all at the same time.

Sitting on the edge of my bed, I open the drawer on my bedside table, and pull the notes out that I had tucked away. I start reviewing the pages of notes that Lauren gave me. The details for the specific dates just seem too coincidental to my travel schedule. I know that all I need to do is proof-source something to know it's all true. If I can't prove anything, then maybe this girl is a nut job like Chad claims.

I typically make big decisions based on information and facts, not emotions. So if I can find proof or documentation of *something* that this Crystal girl said, then I can believe it all.

It wasn't written in the documentation, but one piece of information Lauren mentioned was that the hotels that Chad took Crystal to started out pretty nice but then gradually got lower quality. A recent stay at Crowne Plaza was mentioned, but no date or specific location was outlined.

I take a shot in the dark and call one of the three Crowne Plaza hotels in the Twin Cities.

After a few rings, I hear, "Hello?"

"Hi, this is Mrs. Silver. I need to get a copy of a receipt for a recent stay my husband and I had at your hotel."

"Ok. What was the date of the stay and the name that the reservation was under?"

"October 11, and it's under his name, Chad Silver." I select this date because I felt it in my bones that was the day he cheated. The day I came home from Orlando with shingles and confronted him.

"Ok, just one moment while I look that up for you. Hold, please."

I wait on hold and stare down at my lap, shaking. The entire time, I'm hoping with every ounce of my heart that she's taking so long because there are clearly no records of Mr. Chad Silver staying at that hotel on that date—or any date.

I jolt up with a straight spine when the elevator music stops. She comes back on the line.

She says, "Mrs. Silver? Are you still there?"

"Yes. I'm here."

"Okay, great! I've got that receipt for you right here for your stay on October 11. Where would you like me to email that?"

Sitting on the edge of my bed, my straight spine slumps into a hunched over back, and I somehow recite to her my email address. I clutch my stomach, doubled over in physical pain with a pit in my gut. I feel like I've just been punched and got the wind knocked out of me.

I then wait anxiously with my phone in my hand. I hear the sound of the message with the receipt hit my email and see it come through in my inbox. Ding!

Everything aligns to the fact that he indeed was with Crystal on October 11, just as she described. That's all the proof I need to have confidence that it's all true. Wails leave my mouth in between trying to catch my breath—I'm overcome with devastation. I feel ill.

Oh my God. I think I might puke.

I run to the bathroom and lean over the toilet. Nothing comes out. I collapse into a pile and continue sobbing on the cold, bathroom tile floor.

I eventually climb back into bed. Once I'm able to gain my composure, I call my brother James.

Calling James seems like a strange thing for me to do. Especially because he's barely speaking to me. With him and Karen being separated, he's repeatedly expressed that I should pick his side, even though they still spend a significant amount of time together. He expects me to cut her out of my life after over twenty years because they're moving down a path towards divorce. Because I decline to pick a side, he has all but cut me out of his life.

With little communication between us, I'm out of the loop that he's traveling out of the country and unaware of the time where he is, so I'm lucky to catch him.

When I explain everything to him, he asks, "Do you think there could be some other explanation?" It's the same question he asked back in February when I called him about the lingerie tags. I think he hopes, like me and everyone else, that there's some other reasonable explanation. I'm seeking validation.

My next call is to Lauren.

"Can you come over? I don't want to be alone today." I need her.

While I sit there numb and sensitive, I think about what I'm going to do to occupy myself until she arrives. I can feel nothing, yet I feel everything. Every movement I make feels like I'm going through the motions to simply get by. I feel broken…gutted. My life and heart are completely shattered.

I think about what I need to do to get through the day. I'm

certainly not going to be able to work. I text my boss, "I need to take a personal day today. I'm off tomorrow and Friday, so I'll be out for the rest of the week."

"No problem," he replies.

Next, I pick up the phone to call Karen.

She asks, "What's wrong?"

I'm in hysterics as I tell her, "I'm kicking Chad out and we're breaking up. I just need you to come be here with me after Lauren has to leave."

"What? No you're not." Karen starts laughing. She thinks this is a joke.

"I'm dead serious. I am. We're done," I say adamantly.

"Ok, I'm going out to lunch with some friends and I'll come over later this afternoon."

I look down at my hands and I'm reminded of my nail appointment today. And they look ratchet, so it's a necessity. I'm also scheduled to get the winter tires put on my car.

I drive my car to the dealership, drop it off, and then drive the loaner to my nail appointment.

I'm sitting and staring off into space with my mind reeling the entire manicure. My nail tech is probably wondering what in the hell is going on with me as I sit there like a zombie.

Lauren's already at my house waiting for me when I get home from my nail appointment. She, fortunately, has a job where she can work from home from time to time. We're sitting in the living room, her with her laptop in her lap and me sitting on the couch facing her.

"Did you call the locksmith yet?" Lauren asks.

"No. I'll do that right now." I call the locksmith, and they come quickly to change all of the locks on the house. I know I need to start reclaiming my home and making sure Chad doesn't have any access.

Karen gets there later in the day after her lunch, and the

three of us huddle together in the living room to try to put the pieces together.

Karen says, "I almost drove off the road when you said you were breaking up with him. I was in shock! When you first called, I thought something happened to Emilio."

I think we're all still in shock. I'm not sure any of us can believe that someone would do what Chad's done to me. The three of us are trying to make sense of this horrible situation.

How could he do this? How could he do this to the kids?

What turns out to be even more shocking is that we don't know everything.

Each time I pick up my phone to check, there's still nothing from Chad—no call, no text, no email, no communication whatsoever.

Lauren asks, "What do you think he's going to say? He has to communicate with you at some point!"

I know deep down how he'll respond. "From here on out, it will be nothing but logistics."

WHITE
SKINNY
JEANS

WHEN MY PHONE ALERTS ME that I have a text, the three of us look at each other, eager to know what it says. First, I note that it's 4:38 p.m. FOUR-THIRTY-EIGHT P.M.! Just as I predicted, the first message from Chad comes in, and it's logistical.

This is the first response to my message I sent him at 7:38 a.m., when I sent him a copy of his receipt from his stay with Crystal at the Crowne Plaza in Plymouth, Minnesota. I sent this along with a message with clear instructions that he's no longer allowed in my home and he has five days to get his stuff.

I also shared that he's not welcome alone and gave him two people that he's allowed to accompany him; his friend Mark and his former brother-in-law. These are the only two people that I'm comfortable with him bringing to my home. From what I've learned thus far, I don't trust him. I also don't know how much or how little I know. I have no idea what he's capable of.

I read Chad's text out loud to Lauren and Karen. "It says, 'I need to come get some stuff. Mark will come with me. 6:30 pm ok?'"

"That's it?!" Lauren says, appalled.

"Yep. That's it. I told you I thought it would be all logistics from here on out. I guess we'll see him in a little bit," I say. I acknowledge to Chad via text that it's fine.

Headlights shine brightly, beaming in the darkness down the street around 6:30 p.m. *He's here.* My heart starts pounding out of my chest. There's an aggressive knock on the door. From where I'm sitting on the couch, I can see him through the windows in the front door. While I know it's Chad, I don't recognize the person standing on my doorstep. His eyes are dark with rage beneath the brim of his baseball hat, his face like stone. All I see is a monster knocking on my door. The disdain I feel towards him is indescribable. It's difficult to think that yesterday at this time, I was eager to be wrapped up in his arms. Now, less than twenty-four hours later, the thought of him coming anywhere near me violently repulses me.

When we hear the loud knock, Lauren, Karen, and I all look at each other. *Who's the lucky broad that gets to answer the door?* As we exchange looks, we realize we forgot to draw straws prior to his arrival.

Lauren takes one for the team. She's also the one most equipped to handle him right now. She's sitting in a chair closest to the front door with her back facing it. She slowly stands up and pivots herself on one foot, walks to the door, and slowly cracks it open. She blocks the narrow opening with her body to ensure Chad doesn't get a welcoming impression.

Lauren greets Chad, "What's going on?" in as cordial a tone as possible, considering the current circumstances.

Chad replies, "What do you *mean* what's going on?" in a snarky tone.

"How can I help you?" Lauren meets him with a snarkier tone. I would not want to be on Lauren's shit list.

"Ginny said to come get some stuff."

"No, you told Ginny you needed to come get some stuff. And I think Ginny would be more comfortable if Mark came in rather than you."

"Ginny wants Mark to pick out my clothes?"

The three of us girls had already collected his ugliest items and displayed them for him to gather upon his arrival. This included a spray-painted baseball hat with his name, a 1980s Top-Gun-inspired leather bomber jacket, and his toothbrush... bristles down. Next to his bristles-down toothbrush, I left him some of his empty erectile dysfunction medication packs and a printed copy of his hotel receipt. He's trying to ignore these items, strategically stepping around them while conversing with Lauren.

Lauren replies, "Yep. That's what I said. Ginny would be more comfortable if Mark came inside."

Chad steps back from the door to make room for Mark to enter. Mark timidly enters the house as though he feels he is interrupting something. It's obvious he feels awkward. *Poor guy.*

As Mark's entering my house and Chad is walking away from the door, I hear Lauren shout, "Everything I shared with Ginny is all true. You denying it puts my credibility on the line."

Chad snaps, "No one gives a shit about your credibility, Lauren." The person saying this is unrecognizable to me. The man I've been with for nearly a year and a half—that's been living in my house—would never speak to someone that way. Especially someone that he knows is so important to me.

Mark and I walk back to the closet, where I begin to cry. Mark pulls me in for a big hug.

He says, "I'm so sorry you're hurting. I don't know everything that's going on but I hate seeing you upset."

"It's awful, Mark. I can't believe he would do this to me. Even more so I can't believe that he's doing this to the kids."

I don't want to belabor the conversation with Mark—he is Chad's friend, after all. So we begin selecting Chad's clothes. I help by picking the most ill-fitting and mismatched outfits I can find and shoving them into his fake Louis Vuitton duffle bag. Chad's gained some weight recently, so I make sure to select clothes that he'll really have to squeeze into, like his smallest pair of white skinny jeans.

Moments after Chad speeds away down the street with his bag of white skinny jeans, ugly shirts, and dress shoes, I receive an angry text from him. "How do you expect me to get my stuff if you won't let me in the house?"

I don't feel it's necessary to respond.

It registers that I need to call Elsa and fill her in on what's going on. If Chad can't live with me anymore, neither can the kids. She has the right to know where her children live, and my gut is telling me that Chad isn't chomping at the bit to tell her that he's forty-one years old and homeless.

Elsa doesn't answer when I call her the first time. Or the second time.

When Elsa returns my call, I decide to take the call in my bedroom for privacy away from Lauren and Karen.

"Hi, Elsa. Thank you for calling me back. Sorry to bother you."

"No problem. Is everything ok?"

I'm trying to string my words together through the tears. "Has Chad said anything to you?"

"No. I haven't heard from him at all."

"Okay. Well, I felt like I needed to let you know that we are splitting up and he won't be living here anymore. So Taylor and Logan won't be living here anymore either." I stop to catch my breath.

As I pause, I can hear her let out a deep sigh, and it's not one of relief. I can hear her disappointment.

I continue, "I felt that I needed to bring you up to speed. As their mom, you deserve to know what's going on."

Her mama instincts kick in and she asks, "Is there anything I need to be concerned about regarding the kids?"

YES... THEIR DAD IS A FUCKING PSYCHOPATH, I want to scream. Somehow I maintain my composure. "Well, he certainly doesn't take his role of being a dad very seriously. One thing I know for sure is that on October 11, I was out of town on a work trip. He chose to pawn his children off on you so he could go fuck a girl in a random hotel in the suburbs."

This in itself is substantial to me. It demonstrates the type of parent and person he is, entirely different from the image he attempts to portray.

I sense that Elsa's disturbed, but she doesn't seem surprised.

In fact, she says in a defeated tone, "I remember that night. It was a parent-teacher conference for me and I couldn't take them, so he dropped them off at my sister's, who has five kids and a newborn. Ugh, Ginny. I was afraid this would happen."

What does that mean?

She continues, "I want you to know that it's always given me so much peace knowing that my kids were with you."

I'm shocked to hear her say this. And flattered. A sense of pride sneaks in through all of the hurt and agony. I'm amazed at her grace and I admire her for it. Someday, I hope to be able to have the kind of grace she does.

"I'm so sorry you are going through this." She says this with so much empathy it makes me wonder if she truly understands what I'm going through.

This prompts me to ask, "You don't have to answer this, but did he do this to you?"

After a brief pause, Elsa says, "Yes, he did. Has he admitted any of it to you?"

I say, "Nope."

"That doesn't surprise me. And he probably never will."

"Why do you say that?"

"He'll never admit it because if he did, then what would that make him?" The softness in this statement creates an unexpected intensity.

THE
AFTERMATH:
TRICK-ONOMETRY

LAUREN AND KAREN LEAVE for their respective homes.

I can't eat. I know I need to, but I simply don't have an appetite, and the thought of eating makes me nauseated.

I attempt to go to bed, but my body's under tremendous stress. I can't sleep. I try, but I just lie there and fluctuate between sweating and shivering.

Everything feels out of my control. These feelings are foreign to me. I'm typically in control—of myself and my life, at least. I've never experienced trauma in this manner before.

I'm lying in bed, my mind constantly reeling. I'm racking my brain for memories, replaying these gaps in the relationship, and beating myself up for not believing the doubts I had. I continue trying to put the pieces together.

I fling the covers off out of frustration and decide to put on my proverbial private investigator hat.

I start snooping around in Chad's belongings, searching for more truth and validation.

How bad was this situation I was in?

I become more and more curious. Finally, I discovered his iPad in his bedside table drawer.

Jackpot. Now I just need to get into it.

It's dead. I find the power cord and plug it in. I wait until it has enough juice to power on.

Finally, the little battery light turns green on the screen. The password isn't tough to figure out. I enter the first four digits that come to mind, and the screen lights up and unlocks. The passcode is his birthday.

I opened his email folder, but it hasn't been synced in several months. I start scrolling through the messages, but it's all business-related items.

Where to look next?

I make a note of his Apps and start searching for Hotwire; Lauren shared that Crystal had mentioned he uses that service. No cigar. BUT there is the Hotels.com app. I open the app and find a hotel stay receipt that makes my heart drop into my stomach.

It's the middle of the night, so I can't call or text anyone.

Lauren is going to lose it over this!

I need a break. That's all I can stomach for right now. I close the iPad and go out to the kitchen and get a glass of water, let Emilio outside, and settle in on the couch to wait it out until it's a reasonable time to call Lauren.

I *think* I see the sun coming up, so I text her around 5:30 a.m. "Call me when you're up."

My phone rings immediately. "Hi, you're awake?" I ask.

"Are you kidding? I haven't slept a wink."

"I got into Chad's iPad."

"Oh? What did you find?"

"Well, you know my favorite hotel in Chicago, The Wit?"

"Yep."

"He stayed there with someone while I was away at my national sales meeting in January."

"How do you know he was there with someone?"

"Well, the reservation says two adults. I also called and pretended I was his wife like I did for the Crowne Plaza. They emailed me a copy of the receipt, and it clearly shows that there were two adults under the number of guests. Plus, that whole week I was away, he was saying that he was either with Mark or sick in bed. All the while, he was in Chicago with someone! When I came home from that trip, he had left me flowers, a bottle of champagne, and a card."

"Wow. What a piece of garbage."

"So sick. I guess I need to find a new favorite hotel in Chicago."

"Good idea. What else did you find?"

"Nothing yet. I needed a break after that."

"Have you looked in his notes?" Lauren and I are basically going through his iPad in real time together over the phone.

"No, I hadn't thought about that. Okay, there's a packing list here. Based on the date, it looks like it's from a camping trip with his ex-girlfriend, April," I say.

"Anything interesting on the packing list?"

"Hmm, clothes, supplements, and protein bars. Nothing too out of the ordinary. Wait… Molly? That's not his ex-girlfriend."

"C'mon, Ginny. You don't know what Molly is?"

The light bulb turns on. "Ohhh, you mean like the drug!"

"Yes!"

"Oh! He always said he's super against drugs. That would be crazy. Do you think he does drugs?"

"Well, I certainly wouldn't be surprised. Are you starting to see the pattern of his addictive behavior?"

"I guess I am. It's clear he has a sexual addiction. So, it's not that surprising that he's been hiding other addictions as well."

Something made me think to look at Venmo. I start scrolling through his history. "Lauren?"

"Yes?"

"There are several Venmo transactions that he has labeled as 'strippers and blow' or 'hookers and blow,' and they're public. Do you think he knows that people can see that?"

"He either doesn't know or more likely doesn't care. He might think people think that's cute, but in reality it's probably what it's actually for."

It's starting to add up.

"The women—the lies—the drugs. He tries to portray this image that he's a good dad, a good partner, and a good person. His image is so important to him. All of the posturing must be exhausting. I can't imagine being him and trying to keep up with all of his darkness, deceit and lies."

Lauren and I let all of these new discoveries sink in. We hang up and go about our days.

I'm back on the iPad and on the phone with Lauren.

"Gross. There are all these notes to various women here. Should I read them out loud to you?" I ask Lauren.

"Absolutely."

"Okay, here's the first one… Oh man, it's really sappy and over the top." I start scrolling and pause to read aloud when I get to this line: " 'it created feelings of abandonment.' That's the same shit he used on me when I found those lingerie tags. Oh, here's another good line, 'I'm a good boyfriend, a lover, a supporter, and a caretaker.' "

"According to who?" Lauren guffaws.

"Okay, moving on to the next one. It's to his ex-girlfriend, April. There are a handful of them here addressed to her." I quickly scan them. "Half of them are break-up notes. Oh wow, he's accusing her of being abusive, both verbally and physically."

"Go figure. He would say anything to try to elevate himself," Lauren says flatly.

"Oh, here's a good line, 'I would be so proud to hold your hand walking down the street.' He used a similar line with me at dinner the day after his birthday last year. He said, 'I'm so proud to be seen out in public with you.' Or something along those lines."

"Puke. I don't think I can take any more," Lauren says.

"There are also a lot of comments on all of the therapy he has gone to and work he's done on himself. He never mentioned therapy to me."

"Another lie."

"Ok, one last one. This one is addressed to Elsa."

"What does that one say?"

"Well, it's basically a letter about recommitting to her. It's dated *after* some of these other love letters to April."

"Poor Elsa. Those poor kids. I wonder how twisted her story is."

"I wonder how much she'll be willing to share with me, if anything. Okay, I think that's all we can both handle for right now. I'll keep digging around here and I'll call you if I find anything else interesting."

"Sounds good."

I call Lauren back moments later.

I jump right in as soon as she picks up. "OH MY GOD! There is a *SEX* video in here!"

"Of him?!" Lauren asks.

"Yes! With a woman. And it says last edited May 9. That's right before I took him to Napa. This is a full fourteen-minute video."

"Who's the woman?"

"I have no idea."

"What does she look like?"

"Not like me. She's got a lot of tattoos."

"Can you tell where it is?"

"It looks like it's in his apartment bedroom." *Gut punch.*

"Did you watch the whole thing?"

"Absolutely not! I can't. I couldn't handle more than a couple of minutes. From what I can tell, she seems to know it's being recorded. What's most disturbing is that the kids have access to this iPad! I've seen them on it before. If I can find this, certainly they could, too."

We sit in silence for a moment letting the gravity of this sink in. I continue digging.

There's a screenshot of a coffee shop around this same time in May. I inform Lauren of the find. "He's never mentioned this coffee shop to me. He must've met up with someone there. I can't find any text exchanges here. He must not sync his iPad up with his iMessages."

Who could he have met up with there?

Lauren chimes in, "Remember Crystal said he's been making more time for coffee with her lately? Maybe it was her. I can ask Rachel."

"Ok. Wait. Here is his and Elsa's divorce decree."

"What does that say?"

"Everything looks pretty much as he told me, except the vehicles. He told me that Elsa drove a BMW 5-series when they split, but her car is listed as a Honda CRV. Why lie about that?"

"Who knows what his motivation is for all of his lies. What else?"

"Seems like he had a big chunk of debt that I wasn't aware of."

"No surprises there. Anything interesting in his contacts?"

"Well, here is his ex-girlfriend April's contact information. Should I reach out? I wonder if he pulled the same shit with her."

"Let me know what you decide."

I vacillate back and forth with contradictory thoughts.

Should I reach out to her? Would she be open to talking? Maybe she just wants to forget everything about him.

What's pulling me to reach out to her is a text Chad sent me the day we left for Italy. He was working another seminar when I received this text from him:

"Hi babe. I want you to know my ex-girlfriend is here in attendance. You certainly don't need to be concerned, but I do think it's appropriate to tell you. *Kissy face emoji*" He meant April. April was there.

My blood was boiling. My thought process was that if he was bringing it up, it was an issue for him, which would mean it should be an issue for me. There we were to be leaving on this ten-day elaborate and romantic vacation that night. And he's sending me this message? I took a screenshot of it and sent it to Sara, hoping she would talk me off the ledge.

Instead of Sara telling me I'm an idiot and not to worry about it, she validated how I was feeling. She expressed, "Yeah, I'd be annoyed, too."

I wasn't in a place to be anxious about this. I wanted to be in a good headspace with Chad as we embarked on this amazing vacation. So, I ended up just shoving it deep down, not dealing with it, and heading to Italy.

As I come back into the moment, I ultimately decide to reach out to April.

I send her a simple text explaining who I am and that Chad and his two kids have been living with me for the last six months. That I understand if she has no interest in opening up old wounds and talking to me. She responds within moments and says she'll call me in about twenty minutes, and she's punctual.

April and I introduce ourselves and exchange niceties and condolences. She seems like a reasonable person.

I tell her about the letters I found addressed to her and say, "Do you know that he tells people that you emotionally and physically abused him?"

She laughs and says, "I'm not surprised. He's always trying to paint himself as the victim."

I ask her about the nutrition seminar. "Did you attend a seminar in September that he was at?"

She says, "Yes, I did."

"He sent me a text message that morning saying that you were there but that I didn't have anything to worry about. Did anything happen between you two that weekend?"

"Wow, Chad! Congratulations on telling the truth for once because we aren't fucking anymore! No, I assure you nothing happened between us that weekend."

She also shares with me, "I think Chad is bisexual."

"Really? What makes you think that?"

"Well, about a year and a half ago, he invited me to a swingers party."

"Interesting. Did you go?"

"No! One thing that's always bothered me is that his ex-wife probably thinks I knew he was married. I had no idea until long after we split up."

"We've been in communication quite a bit, and we're getting together next week to sit down and go through some things."

"Will you please tell her that I had no clue? I just feel like that might give her some peace. Us women need to stick together and support each other"

"I absolutely will share that with her. And I wholeheartedly agree."

We hang up, and I dig back into Chad's iPad, where I find more of his hidden apps, like Snapchat.

Isn't that for teenagers?

I find an app that I've never heard of before called Wickr. I research it and discover that it's an adult chatting site. Perhaps that's the app he used to keep conversations with Crystal and other women hidden.

HINDSIGHT

THE INVESTIGATIONS CONTINUE. I'm on the phone with Sara now.

"I need you to do me a huge favor," I say.

"Anything. What can I do?" Sara asks.

"Will you please call the Nicollet Island Inn in Minneapolis and see if Chad had a stay there any time in the fall?" I'm a bit hesitant. I know this is a big ask.

"You got it. I don't know how I'm going to do it, but I'll figure it out," she says.

Sara doesn't waste any time. She handles the task and calls me back within fifteen minutes.

"I pretended I was his assistant." She beams with pride at her creativity.

"Oh, good idea! And?"

"There was nothing. They couldn't find any stays under his name for any dates in recent history."

"Interesting. Okay, well thank you for doing that. I really appreciate it." I feel a little deflated. I get a little rush every time more evidence stacks up, and I thought this one was a sure thing, but we came up empty.

As I continue trying to put the puzzle pieces together and fill in the gaps, my mind drifts back to that October day when I was entertaining Taylor and Logan at the mall.

Leading up to that weekend, Chad had told me, "I got us a hotel room at the JW Marriott so we can stay the night if we want to."

I remembered thinking that was a bit odd because it's only ten minutes away from his apartment, and that's also supposed to be time with the kids.

It dawns on me that maybe he never canceled the hotel room. Instead, I bet he was using it with someone else while the kids and I were looking for him.

In an attempt to confirm my suspicions, I pick up the phone and call the hotel. I've become an expert at calling hotels as Mrs. Silver to retrieve copies of hotel receipts. I'm put on hold for a moment. Then the operator comes back on the phone and says they were able to locate the hotel receipt and will happily send it over for "our" stay.

I knew it!

I called Lauren to give her the most recent updates. "There's no record of him staying at the Nicollet Island Inn, but I did get a copy of the receipt from the JW Marriott last year. Remember when I had the kids and he was nowhere to be found? He had to have been in the hotel room! I wonder with whom?"

"Do you want me to reach out to Rachel and see if it was Crystal?"

"Sure. If you don't mind."

"It wasn't her. She didn't go there with him last year. It also wasn't Crystal that went to that coffee shop that you found the screenshot of back in May. She was dating someone else then and wasn't speaking to Chad. She did confirm that it was the same hotel he invited her to this year, but she canceled because she found out about you."

"Ugh! He practically begged me to come have lunch with him there on my way to the airport and I did! Okay, so we've confirmed it wasn't her at the coffee shop, the JW Marriott or theWit. Who knows who these other women, or people, are." His behavior is deplorable.

I continue, "I just thought of something else. If he's been leaving home for the entire night while I'm away on work trips, that means Emilio has been left alone for who knows how many hours!"

"Yeah, you're right. What kind of person would do that to a dog? They can't fend for themselves. Not to mention that Emilio needs extra attention and care."

"And what about when Sadie was sick with cancer? This might be one of the most egregious and upsetting things he's done yet. I was with someone that's an animal abuser. I can't believe he would neglect a dog. My dogs are my babies!"

My heart breaks again, this time for Sadie and Emilio.

STIRRUPS

THE FLUORESCENT LIGHTS ARE BLINDING as they beam down from the generic white tiles of the ceiling. The paper underneath me is crisp and rustles uncomfortably every time I dare to move a muscle. Friday morning starts out with me naked from the waist down in a room with Christine. She's the sweet nurse at the urgent care center.

I don't remember how I got here. I know I drove myself, but my mind is such a mess that it's taking every ounce of energy and brainpower to put one foot in front of the other.

As Christine enters the room and introduces herself, she asks me, "What brings you in today?"

I immediately burst into tears as I began to explain to her why I'm here. The words feel surreal as they come out of my mouth. "My boyfriend of nearly a year and a half, who lived with me and whose children I've been parenting, has been cheating on me the entire time. And I've confirmed that he doesn't use protection. So I need to be tested for every STD, including HIV."

She asks me to scoot my naked behind to the edge of the table and put my feet in the stirrups. While this is generally an uncomfortable position to fold your body into at each annual exam, the shame I feel during this moment is insurmountable. Never did I imagine I'd be in this position, both literally and figuratively.

Finding out that Chad didn't use protection with Crystal was frightening in itself, but it also made me realize that he likely didn't use protection with the other people he was frolicking around with. That means he's been putting my physical health at risk.

I feel humiliated.

Mortified.

Angry.

Devastated.

Dirty.

All of these feelings are stirring around inside me as I'm lying on the medical bed half-naked.

Christine is kind, gentle, and understanding. She completes the examination and then leaves the room to allow me to get dressed.

When she comes back into the room, she informs me, "You have bacterial vaginosis." I'm again flooded with humiliation and fear. My second diagnosis in two-months.

"What does that mean? What is that?"

Christine says, "It usually goes away without treatment in ninety percent of nonpregnant women."

"I'm not pregnant, am I?" I ask with serious concern.

"No, you're not pregnant," she says reassuringly.

"Okay, that's a relief." I release a gigantic exhale. I realized I'd been holding my breath. That would have been an impossible scenario. I'm dealing with enough here.

"So I wouldn't recommend treatment unless you start to have symptoms." she explains.

We opt to see if it will go away on its own. I go home and do what any normal person would do... I Google that shit.

Now, I think I'd generally be considered a pretty cool, calm, and collected person by most, except when it comes to health.

What stands out most to me when I Google "bacterial vaginosis" is that it's most common in women with new or multiple sexual partners. There have been no new partners here –I've been loyal. I never strayed once. When would I have time, even if I wanted to? This is all making sense since *he* has been engaging with multiple partners. Maybe Google should add *that*!

I find myself back at the clinic a few weeks later. Unfortunately for me, the symptoms decided to materialize. I need a prescription medication to treat it. There are some potentially strong side effects of this drug, which means no alcohol—for a WEEK. Talk about adding salt to an open wound!

Mercifully, this is the only diagnosis I receive. But this is a huge wake-up call for me. I take my health and wellness seriously, and I believe everyone can benefit from doing the same. From this moment forward, I know I'll be taking extra precautions and will be hypervigilant in conversations with any potential future partner.

ANNE & LOU

WHEN I GET HOME FROM THE CLINIC, I send Lou a message saying, "I'm so sad to not get to work out with you. *Heartbreak emoji*"

And she responds, "Me too!"

She calls me after their training session with Chad. Lou's extremely confused and conflicted. "Ok, that was weird," Lou starts in.

"What has he told you?" I ask.

Lou says, "Chad told me and Anne that he's being framed. He's adamant that this girl is crazy and that she's trying to black-mail him!"

My response is, "And what exactly is she trying to blackmail him for? His sweet orange leather sofa?"

She laughs and says, "Ginny, it's so strange. I told him, 'Chad, I am willing to help you. I will do whatever it takes to help you prove to Ginny that this girl is blackmailing and framing you.

She can't do this to you. I will help you show Ginny!' And that's when things took a turn."

"What do you mean things took a turn?"

Lou continues, "Chad snapped. He yelled at me and said, 'I don't need that kind of help, Lou! I just need your support. I'm in crisis mode and need to find somewhere to live.' Anne and I slowly turned and looked at each other. We both knew something was off. We connected in the parking lot afterward and agreed that things weren't adding up. I asked Anne, 'What do you think?' Anne said, 'I don't know, Lou. Something seems off. I have to tell you that I've heard from a reliable source that Chad's relationship with April, his last girlfriend, ended poorly.'"

"I actually talked to her yesterday. It was quite interesting to hear her perspective," I say.

"You did? Oh, I'd love to hear what she had to say. Why don't you come have lunch with me today and get out of the house?" Lou insists. She tells me where and what time to meet her.

I sit down to lunch with Lou and realize she's invited another friend of hers that I've never met. I'm not particularly interested in sharing the extremely personal, intimate, horrible details of my life with a new person.

Clearly Lou has filled her in somewhat about what's going on, which makes me feel very uncomfortable. It becomes clear during the conversation that Lou is still on the fence. She's having a difficult time believing that Chad could do all of these awful things we're learning. Lou's a fixer, and she thinks she can help him—if what he says is true.

I have my armamentarium of documentation to ensure that she knows everything is true. I brought the hotel receipts. I even brought the Crowne Plaza linen spray bottle that I confiscated from his overnight bag, along with the rest of my evidence.

I also brought his iPad. I'm confident that I still haven't

discovered everything yet. However, there's that sex video. To help paint a literal picture for Lou, I go ahead, without warning, and hit play and turn the video on for her.

She says, "Uggh! I'm going to be scarred forever. I can't unsee his bare ass!"

I think this moves Lou to my side of the fence.

After lunch, I'm home waiting for Lou and Karen to arrive to begin packing up Chad's belongings when I receive a text from Anne. "I'm so very very sorry; my heart has been heavy all day. Big hugs to you."

I'm relieved to hear from her because it validates our friendship. We make plans to get together for coffee on Sunday.

Once Lou and Karen arrive, the three of us begin packing up Chad's possessions. It takes a total of about three hours. We could have done it faster, but we had to give the packing some extra attention to detail.

We used some boxes and bags I had to pack up Chad's clothes. To maximize resources, we fill his royal blue hard-sided suitcases with clothes.

I research a few therapists that specialize in sex addiction around the Twin Cities area. I print off their contact information. We tape those to the outside of his suitcase very securely. I hold the tape, and Lou spins the suitcase around and around and around. We don't want it to get lost—it's important that he receives this information.

There's also his overnight duffle bag that we fill with items. We empty out all of his erectile dysfunction medication foil packs and flush the pills down the toilet. The empty packs get attached to the top of his duffle bag with packing tape that encompasses the bag several times.

I'm heading downstairs when Karen says, "I want to see the sex video."

Oooookaaayy. "What? Why?"

"Well, if he's getting all these women, I want to see what all the fuss is about."

I give her the passcode to the iPad and go downstairs to keep packing with Lou. After several minutes, Lou asks, "Where's Karen?"

"She wanted to see the sex video. I thought she'd be down here by now. I'll go check on her."

I walk upstairs, and Karen's still watching the porno. She's watching the entire thing! She slides out of the chair to the floor onto her knees and starts thrusting her hips, mimicking Chad in the video.

"That's gross, Karen," I say. I'm utterly appalled.

I see her tense up and it's obvious my reaction pisses her off.

"It's just too soon. Someday it might be funny, but my life feels like it's in shambles right now, and I just kicked this guy out two days ago," I say in an attempt to gain a little compassion.

She shuts down and barely speaks to me the rest of the day, although she stays to help finish packing.

Downstairs, I power on the TV in the kid cave for a little background noise while we're packing. When the screen lights up, the apps are still logged into Chad's accounts. We open up one of the apps, and the first movie that pops up on his watchlist is *Leaving Las Vegas*. Lou and I look at each other in horror. I switched over to his Netflix account and found a show about call girls and a show about escorts, in addition to *50 Shades of Gray*.

"This is what the kids have had access to on their TV?!" I exclaim.

Lou agrees, "That is not something kids that age should be watching." We're all beginning to become numb to the shock of what we're finding.

Lou and I try to lighten the mood and continue with our shenanigans of incorporating a little fun while packing. We find a book of Chad's, *The Guide to Good Relationships*. We tear out the title page, and I write "Good read??" on it and tape that to the top of a box. These are a few of the fun little gems we'll leave for him to discover during his move.

While I'm thankful it didn't take long, it's also a little bit of a sad reality. We haul his orange leather sofa to the garage. We carry the drum set, a love seat, a bookshelf, and a couple of chairs to join the sofa. The rest is clothes and personal belongings and a few boxes of kitchen items.

Although I'm mentally, emotionally, and physically exhausted, it's another sleepless night.

CRYSTAL
CLEAR

ON SATURDAY MORNING, I open my bathroom drawer, where I keep my makeup. It's not there. I look in the other drawers and come up empty.

Where the heck could my makeup be? Oh yes—in my suitcase, in my car, at the dealership. Convenient.

I'd completely spaced that I had dropped my car off and had a loaner.

I'm standing at the bathroom vanity when my phone rings. I'm trying to make myself somewhat presentable before going to the dealership to retrieve my suitcase. I'm attempting to add some body and volume to my baby-fine hair with the curling iron. *At least my hair will be done.* I look down and see it's Lauren calling. I set the iron down on the counter to answer the phone.

"Hey," I answer. I'm a little distracted as I'm thinking about how I'm going to make everything work out from a timing standpoint this morning now that I have to unexpectedly drive to the dealership.

"Hey. I know that today, of all days, is not your day to have to pay it forward. But you're going to. Crystal and Rachel are going to come by your house at 9:30 this morning to meet you. I'll be there, too. You're going to help give Crystal closure so that she can see how strong you are and hopefully give her some confidence to move on with her life."

"Okay." I'm not answering a question, but agreeing to a statement.

I walk into my home from retrieving my makeup bag to see Crystal, Rachel, and Lauren sitting in my living room drinking coffee. Crystal sees me and instantly falls apart and starts crying.

Meeting Crystal makes me realize that we could not be more different. It's difficult to decipher if her mild-mannered meekness has always been a characteristic of hers or if her confidence has simply been broken due to the circumstances with Chad. I am doing the best I can to hold it together as the man and children that I believed I'd be spending the rest of my life with as a family are moving out of my house. She's crying. I'm not, and seeing her like this makes me feel like I can't break down. Lauren and I are counseling her on having the strength to resist falling back into his trap if, and when, he reaches out again.

"Your home is beautiful," Crystal says, looking around once she's able to compose herself.

"Thank you."

"If it helps at all, he never told me that he loved me and he never let me meet his kids, even though I wanted to. I asked several times," Crystal explains. "Chad had one of his friends call me and tell me that everything Chad said is true. That Logan does have brain cancer. He told me, 'Chad's a good guy. Just hang in there.'"

She even says Logan's name. This shakes me to my core.

He talks about the kids—the ones that have been living with me in my house, that I've been caring for, and carpooling, and loving— with these other women?!

This makes me feel sick to my stomach.

"He said that Logan has brain cancer?!" I ask in shock and disgust.

"Yes, he said that's one of the main reasons he couldn't tell you about me when I kept pressuring him. He said that they needed your health insurance."

"They're not even on my health insurance. The kids are on their mom's health insurance. And what kind of parent would make up that their kid has brain cancer—or any type of cancer for that matter? Why would you even put that out into the universe?"

"So, there's no brain cancer?" Crystal asks hesitantly.

"Absolutely not. No one has brain cancer," I assure her.

"He was crying about it over the phone when he was in Chicago recently."

"You mean when he was in Chicago with me?"

The cat seems to have gotten Crystal's tongue.

I continue, getting back to the subject at hand, "I bet it was Kevin that called. I can't think of anyone else that would corroborate such awful lies."

She leans forward in the chair and says, "I thought I recognized Kevin's voice. I actually made out with him once a long time ago. We had each other's phone numbers and had communicated some in the past. When he called, it was a blocked number, but I thought I recognized his accent and voice; you're right. It was totally Kevin."

I wish Crystal well and encourage her to stay strong as we wrap the conversation up so Lauren and I can prepare for Chad to retrieve his things.

Shortly after they leave, about ten of my friends come to support me and watch Chad gather his belongings from my garage. We pop bottles of bubbly and eat snacks, attempting to make a celebration out of me moving forward with my life.

One of my guy friends, Dustin, is a former professional athlete. He has a muscular stature and a strong presence. Having him there will intimidate Chad.

Up until the last moment, Chad keeps trying to gain control. As he and a couple of Kevin's helpers are on their way, he texts me, "You can pop the garage door so we can back the truck up into the driveway."

I don't respond, and I also don't open the garage door. Nope. I'm not going to do a goddamn thing that he instructs me to do. I'm going to show him that I've regained control and I'm the boss.

I ask Dustin to walk outside with me to greet them. My makeup is on point. My washed, blow-dried, and curled hair blows slightly in the wind. I'm wearing my best pair of skinny jeans, sky-high boots, and a leopard-print silk shirt. All of this is topped with my new long, black puffy coat I recently purchased on our Chicago trip.

As we approach the guys that'll be moving the stuff, I have the garage door opener in my coat pocket. I'm striding in the most commanding manner I can muster, even though I'm shaking from head to toe and my hands and feet feel numb—partly from the adrenaline and partly from the cold.

We walk towards them, and I motion to one side of the garage as I say, "All of his belongings are on the floor on this side of the garage. There's also some patio furniture around the back of the house. If you have any questions on what you should touch or not touch, you may direct those to me." I hit the button on the garage door opener in my pocket, and the door began to rise.

Chad immediately scurries around the back of the house to start grabbing patio furniture. Most likely to avoid me.

Chad never looks me in the eyes today. He doesn't even dare to look at me. Not once. After everything is packed up, I send him off with one last parting gift.

As I walk out into the garage and down the two stairs with Dustin by my side to meet him and Mark face to face, I casually hand him his iPad. I make sure to have his sex video playing on full volume as I hand it over. While displaying the screen towards him, I say, "I thought you'd appreciate having your iPad back."

He quickly slams the cover shut, but the sound keeps playing, and you can hear the echoing of the moans blasting from the speaker. He's frantically pressing the buttons on the side trying to turn the volume down without having to re-open the iPad cover to expose the visual of the video.

Of all days, I don't cry a single tear today.

HAIRY
SITUATIONS

AS I WALK UP THE STAIRS to Anne's house on Sunday morning,
I take a few deep breaths. I know I need to prepare myself to
rehash all of this horrible information once again. Every time I
talk about it, it's like reliving it.

Anne greets me with a huge hug, and I immediately start
sobbing. After she brews us some fresh coffee, we sit down in
the living room.

"How are you?" Anne asks with genuine concern.

"Not great, but I'm putting one foot in front of the other."

"What in the hell happened, Ginny?"

"Well, that's kind of a loaded question. A lot. How much
do you want to know?"

Anne says, "As much as you're willing to share."

"I am willing to tell you as much or as little as you want. It
comes with a warning that it's extremely disturbing, and it will

change your opinion of Chad. Let me know if you're prepared for that, and I will start from the beginning."

Anne nods to go ahead, and I do just that. I share with Anne everything I know up until this point while she listens with shock and concern.

"Oh my God, Ginny. I am so sorry. This is awful. I'm never going back there."

"Look, I'm not trying to get anyone to take sides or pull you away from working out there."

"Are you kidding me? I would never want to be associated with someone like that or support their business. Plus, did Lou tell you that he had the audacity to charge our credit cards for our session on Friday when we never even worked out?"

"What? That's terrible! Do you feel comfortable with someone like that having access to your credit card on file?"

"No! Lou and I decided that we are both canceling our credit cards. That's theft. He's a fraud!" I could see the wheels turning. "So, where are we going to work out moving forward?"

"We'll figure it out," I say, comforted by the idea of continuing a workout regimen with Anne and Lou.

"To be honest, I've looked at switching gyms many times in the past."

"Oh really? Why?"

"He would cancel our sessions at the last minute all the time. There would be times when Lou and I would be sitting in the parking lot and would get a text from him canceling our workout."

"Wow, that's awful. So you'd drive all the way down there for no reason. That's shitty."

"Yeah. And then you came into the picture and things have been the most consistent they've ever been. Now we know why there's been so much unreliability with him over the years."

It's been five days since my life unraveled. As I try to get back to living, I look at my calendar at what's ahead. I see the family photo session scheduled for the week of Thanksgiving. *I'll need to cancel that.*

Next, I notice the day I scheduled for the four of us to volunteer at the food bank. *I'll need to let them know that we won't be attending.*

In the immediate future, I have to travel to Denver for work tomorrow for an important customer dinner that one of my colleagues, Owen, and I are co-hosting. He was in Minneapolis last week, and we were supposed to have lunch last Wednesday, but I canceled at the last minute. He'd been sending me text messages and tried calling me, but I haven't responded.

I text Owen, "I'm so sorry I fell off the face of the earth. The short story is that my life fell apart and I needed to take a few days off of work. I haven't slept or eaten much in almost a week. I'll be there tonight, but I need to ask you to take the lead. I hope that's not too much to ask. I'm not ready to talk about it yet, but I'll fill you in at some point."

He replies immediately, "I've got your back. No questions asked."

I fly to Denver, put my best game face on, and manage to make it through dinner. No one has a clue what's going on. On the outside, I appear completely fine and can have a productive business discussion over dinner.

In an attempt to make light conversation outside of business talk, one of our customers turns their attention to me. "So, Ginny, is there an important man in your life?"

I set my fork down and sit up tall in an attempt to maintain my composure and say with the best grin I can conjure, "No, there isn't."

Owen shoots me a knowing glance and saves the day with a diversion by raising his glass. "I'd like to make a toast. Thank you to everyone for coming out tonight. We appreciate all that you've done, and we know that the future is bright. Cheers!"

On the inside, I'm completely broken. I feel supported by my colleague, but this scenario is so much more than what's going on with me. Just because someone appears to have it all together, you never know what is going on in their life. We've all heard the saying, "You can't judge a book by its cover."

This is reflective of the relationship I thought I was in. Chad had been posturing his entire life to make people believe he's someone he isn't. He also did the same as it relates to the relationship with me. Everyone thought that we were this happy couple and family, including me. Understanding that you never really know what's going on from the outside never rang more true than in this pivotal moment, at a work dinner, and it began to change my outlook.

After dinner commences, Owen and I thank everyone and say our goodbyes. We walk straight to the bar to debrief over a cocktail.

"Thank you for taking the lead tonight. I really appreciate it," I say to Owen.

"Hey, don't mention it. You'd do the same for me."

"I hope I wasn't too much of a mess."

"No one had a clue that anything's going on with you. You did great. I wouldn't have even known if you hadn't told me something was up."

"Okay, that's good to hear."

"Care to share?"

"Not yet. It's too fresh. Thank you for asking, though, and for having my back. It means a lot."

We finish our drinks, and I go back to my empty hotel room before I fly home to my empty house in the morning.

I have a hair appointment scheduled in anticipation of our family photos. While I canceled the photo session, I didn't cancel my appointment with my hairstylist... the stylist that Chad, Lou, and I all share.

As I sit down in the chair and we get started, I inform her that Chad and I broke up.

"What happened?" she asks with big eyes as she takes a step back.

"Are you sure you want to know?" And I continue with my disclaimer. I'm hoping just a little bit that she'll say no since things are still fresh and difficult to talk about. I'm getting a little fatigued.

"Yes, I'm sure." She wants to know everything, so I give her the details. I see tears in her eyes right along with mine.

I'm surprised to hear her respond with, "I never liked or trusted him from the first time I met him." She says this while shaking her head in disgust from side to side.

"What?" I'm shocked.

"Yes! But then I met you, and I thought that I must have been wrong about him! He had to be a decent guy. I mean, *you* were with him!"

We both shake our heads in disbelief.

When Lou later shares with me that Chad's still going to this stylist, I decide that I need to move on and make my next appointment with someone I've seen several times over the years.

THANKSGIVING

THE WEEK OF THANKSGIVING IS A WHIRLWIND. Elsa and I meet for happy hour. I have a stack of documentation that I feel she needs to see and information she needs to hear. The more I'm learning, the more I realize that I don't know Chad at all. I had no idea that he was capable of all of the things he's done. Which means I have no idea what he's capable of. And I feel a duty to protect these children that I love.

As Elsa and I sit down, I begin to tee up the conversation and give her a glimpse of everything that I've found so far so she has a full understanding of the severity of the situation.

Just as Elsa and I are about to dive into the details of our horrid stories, the server walks up to the table and asks her "What can I get for you?"

"That glass of red wine looks delicious and necessary," she says, pointing to mine. "I'll have what she's having."

I offered her some of my french fries that I'd ordered while waiting for her to arrive. I pop a fry in my mouth as she begins.

Elsa says, "One day, I was walking to the bus stop to pick up Taylor after kindergarten. I received a call from a phone number I didn't recognize. I answered, and there was a man on the phone. He said, 'Your husband is fucking my wife.' I was stopped in my tracks."

I'm taken back because the way she shares this makes me feel her pain from that moment. Plus, Elsa doesn't use language like that. "What did you say?"

"I asked him, 'What? Who is this?' I was completely blind-sided and thought it couldn't be true. I thought he had the wrong phone number. He didn't. I learned he was referring to a woman he worked with at the gym where he was employed. She was pregnant. I don't think she was technically married to him, but he ordered a paternity test. The results determined that the baby wasn't Chad's, thankfully."

Elsa continues, "This relationship turned out to be so problematic that Chad eventually got fired from said gym, according to someone that shared this with me later on. It was also such a big problem for this man that he decided to pick up his family and move them to Arizona to get away from Chad. Apparently, when I believed Chad was going to work in the mornings, he would drive to her house, would sit in his car outside their home in the morning, and wait for him to go to work. When Chad would see the car pull out of the driveway, he would pull his car into the garage."

"Elsa, this is Jerry Springer-level stuff!" I exclaim in a hushed tone.

"I know. I confronted him, and he denied everything. After I finally pinned him in a corner with evidence, he agreed to start counseling to try to save our marriage."

"You know what's interesting—Chad had a work trip to Arizona when we first started dating," I share.

"I wouldn't be surprised if he saw her. Anyway, after I thought things had gotten better, I saw Chad's laptop open on the coffee table. Curiosity got the best of me, and I found emails between those two. They said terrible things about me. They even had a nickname for me. They called me 'The Undesirable.' All of the messages were very sexual and graphic."

Elsa goes on, "Chad would send me to the spa for the entire day. Trust me, we couldn't afford it. This put me in a position to be busy and not available by phone for the day. On those days, he would fly to Arizona early in the morning, have sex with this woman, and then fly back in time to be home with his family for dinner. He was spending money on these trips while our financial situation meant we were putting groceries on credit cards."

"That must have been extremely difficult to come to grips with," I say empathetically.

"That's not even the worst of it. He has this fake email account where I found a lot of dark stuff on his computer, including that he was going to massage parlors for sexual pleasure. It was like stuff out of the back of the City Pages. Remember the City Pages, Ginny?" These are things no wife wants to find in her husband's computer. "It was a terrible time. It made me feel so awful about myself, like something was wrong with me. We had so little intimacy, it's a miracle that we have two children. That's not what I thought marriage was going to be."

"First of all, you are not the one that there's anything wrong with. Truly, if there's anything that comes from this terrible situation, I hope that it helps give you reassurance. I don't want this to open up old wounds for you. I hope that it's more helpful than anything."

"It's been a journey, and I'm finally starting to heal. For so long, I thought that I was broken, but being able to share this with you does help."

The server stops by to check on us, and we order a second glass of wine. This conversation definitely warrants a second glass of wine.

Elsa lets out a little frustration, "Argh! I cannot believe Chad messed this up with you. He had *everything* with you."

"He had everything with you, too."

"Taylor and Logan have been asking when they can see you. Would you be open to that? I hope that's not awkward."

"It's not awkward at all! When they came into my life, I thought it was forever. I'll always make time for them as long as they still want to have a relationship with me. I miss them terribly. I'd love to see them."

We establish right then how important it is to never say anything negative about Chad to or in front of the kids. It's a little pact we make. Despite what he's done, he's their father, and we agree no good will come of them learning about his darker side. I'm sensing we're forming a bond.

"How about if you come over on Sunday afternoon?"

"That sounds great. I'll see you then."

FRANCINE

KAREN MADE ME DO IT. Seeing as Chad and I already had the appointment with the breeder set for the Sunday after Thanksgiving, she said that I still need to go. "It will be good for you," she said.

I show up at the appointment, and the poor breeder looks somewhat confused.

"Is it just… you?" She asks, looking out the door in the distance to see if there's anyone else with me.

"Yep, it's just me," I say surely as I prepare to step through the doorway into her home.

I'm hopeful that she has so many conversations with potential buyers that she thinks she's confused me with someone else. I don't want to get into the details.

The breeder doesn't have any puppies available or "for sale." There are three puppies that are ten days old and three puppies that are five months old that she's keeping for herself as show dogs to add to her collection. They're gorgeous!

There are four different colorings for Cavalier King Charles Spaniels; blenheim, black and tan, tricolor, and ruby. Two of the five-month-old puppies are blenheim, and one is ruby.

I do believe that there's something to be said about pets picking us just as much as we pick them and ending up with the unexpected.

I think back to when I got Sadie. I was confident and determined that I would be getting a boy. This was perfect because the breeder I was visiting had eight puppies; seven boys and one girl. When I looked at the first litter of five boys, none were calling to me. When the three others came trotting out, I pointed to the little white fluff ball and said, "That's the one." The breeder simply replied, "That's the girl." And just like that… I went home with a girl.

When I meet the Cavalier King Charles Spaniel puppies that Sunday after Thanksgiving, the ruby-colored girl is clinging to me. I have to have her, and she has to have me. She has the most perfect personality, and I want to save her from her bully sisters. She's what some people call the runt of the litter. I like to call her petite.

I call the breeder that afternoon as I'm driving to see the kids at Elsa's. The phone rings over my Bluetooth speaker in the car.

The breeder answers, and I say, "Hi, this is Ginny. I was at your house earlier today. I simply cannot stop thinking about that ruby. I never would have pictured myself with a ruby, but there is something about that puppy that I'm very drawn to. I feel strongly that I need her and she needs me."

Her name is Elizabeth. I don't want to call her that because I know I'll change it since it doesn't seem to fit her.

The breeder says, "Thank you for calling and saying that. Sometimes these are the types of conversations that help me make a decision. There are several people involved in the process that I'll need to consult with. It will take me a couple of weeks to contact everyone involved to decide if we can let her go."

So I wait. After we hang up, I drive the rest of the way to Elsa's in silence so I can gather my thoughts. I'm still in so much pain, but I need to push that aside to focus on Taylor and Logan right now.

When I arrive at Elsa's to see the kids for the first time since the split, I'm having an incredibly difficult time controlling my emotions and composure. While my emotional faucet for Chad was shut off immediately, my emotions and love for Taylor and Logan still flow freely. They've never seen me broken and crying like this before. I'm grateful to see them, but also scared and nervous.

How do I convey that I love them immensely while telling them they can't live with me anymore?

I squeeze them tight, and they squeeze me back. This is the longest we've ever gone without seeing each other since we met. We sat down in the living room. Our seating arrangement is a little out of place as Logan clings to Elsa and Taylor snuggles in next to me.

Elsa and I had decided to sit down together and talk to the kids. I'd rehearsed what I wanted to say to them to express how important they were to me.

I wondered, *What has Chad told them? Has he been honest? Has he tried to make me look like the bad guy? I still want to be in the kids' lives, but will they still want to have a relationship with me? How will we navigate things moving forward?*

As we get settled, Elsa sets down a box of tissues on the coffee table. I grab a handful, knowing I'll need them, and begin my speech.

Through tears, I manage to get out, "It's important that you both know that when I made a commitment to be in a relationship with your dad, it was just as much of making a commitment to you two."

I take a deep breath.

"I made a commitment to the four of us being a family." I pause to wipe my eyes. "You know that, right?"

"Yeah, we know." They say, nodding slowly after looking between me and Elsa to assure it's okay to speak up and express their feelings.

"Although your dad and I won't be together anymore, that doesn't change my commitment to you or how much I love you." I take another moment to wipe my tears and the snot dripping from my nose before continuing.

"I planned to be at your high school and college graduations. I planned to be at your weddings."

This clearly strikes Elsa. She locks eyes with me and chimes in, "And you still will." She squeezes Logan by her side.

Taylor looks up at me from my side and says with a bit of frustration, "But I don't understand."

"What don't you understand, Baby?" Elsa asks.

"You seem so sad," Taylor replies, still looking up at me.

"I *am* sad."

"And Dad is sad. You're both sad. We're all sad. This doesn't make any sense!" Now the frustration is really on display.

Before I respond, I have to consider how confusing this must be to them at their ages. They're still so innocent, and this is a lot to process. Even though my heart is shattered into a million pieces, my job is to protect their little hearts. And here I am feeling guilty because I'm left feeling helpless to do so in this impossible situation.

"I know, Sweetheart. It's hard to make sense of it all. But what's most important is that you know that I will always be here for you and love you no matter what."

After we get through the hard part, Logan asks, "Mom, can Ginny stay and help us put up the Christmas tree?"

"If she has time. Of course she's welcome to stay," Elsa says, looking at me, and asks me directly, "Would you like to stay?"

"I would love to."

The breeder reaches out a week later, to my delight, and tells me the ruby girl, who I name Francine, is mine. Early December, she comes home and fills my heart more than I could have ever imagined.

MODERN
FAMILY

ELSA TELLS ME OVER THE PHONE, "Taylor asked if they can stay with you every Monday."

"What did you say?"

"I said I'm not changing our custody arrangement. And that's a lot to ask of you."

"Well, I'd be happy to have them. How did it go over when you said no?"

"Then they asked for every other Monday. Ha!"

They're persistent! It fills my heart that they want to continue having me as part of their regular routine.

Because Elsa clearly isn't going to change her custody schedule to include me in it, we compromise with them and say that they're always welcome to see me and stay over whenever it works out for them, me, and Elsa.

I'm snuggled in and hunkered down with Taylor and Logan. They're here for an overnight on this cold December Monday.

They're having a tough time with the split, and both are feeling a little down, craving one-on-one time with me. On this particular night, Taylor's hanging out upstairs, and Logan's watching TV downstairs. So I'm alternating up and down between having some alone time with each of them.

I'm downstairs with Logan when the doorbell rings. I look at my watch—8:52 p.m. Who is at the door at 8:52 p.m. on a Monday night? If I were home alone, I probably wouldn't have answered. I don't yet have a video security doorbell installed. So to see who's at the door, the door has to physically be opened.

Taylor yells down, "Ginny, someone's at the door!" So I hustle up the stairs, two at a time, and answer the door with Taylor standing right behind me.

There's a man at the door. "I'm looking for Chad Silver."

I state, "Umm… He doesn't live here any longer."

"Do you know where I can find him? I'm a process server and need to serve him with some legal documents."

Immediately, my instincts kick in, and I'm in child protection mode. Taylor is eager to provide the name of Chad's new apartment building where he's living in downtown Minneapolis. I step outside with Francine in my arms and close the door.

I say, "Look, these are his kids. Can we not do this in front of them?"

He asks, "Are you his ex?"

"Yes."

"I'm sorry, ma'am. I won't take any more of your time. Have a good night." I can't tell if he's apologizing for the fact that I'm his ex or that he feels like he's intruding.

I shut the door and think, *What just happened? What the hell did Chad do to cause someone to hunt him down with legal documents?*

EMPTY
MIDDLE
SEAT

AS CHRISTMAS APPROACHES, the realization that my life is not what I thought it would be continues to slap me in the face. Everything changed in a blink of an eye, and it still catches me off guard from time to time.

Elsa and I agree that I can take the kids to celebrate Christmas with them on December 22. Then, we decided that she should come, too. We're enjoying a home-cooked meal at my house. Then we open gifts, play games, put together Lego sets, and celebrate.

The four of us are sitting on the ground, gathered around the coffee table playing a game. With the warmth of the fire and the sound of Christmas music playing, everything seems just as it should.

Elsa looks around and takes in the environment before

saying, "I am good with having a modern family like this. We all came into each other's lives for a reason."

I smile and say, "I feel the same way."

"It's important to me to teach Taylor and Logan that people aren't disposable. This is the perfect way to show them that relationships have value and people matter."

"I couldn't agree more."

Elsa and I engage in some conversation and the most recent updates about Chad as we enjoy some wine. As I'm taking a sip of mine, I contemplate what the difference is that I see in Elsa. Once I put my finger on it, I say, "You know, I think you've gotten some swagger back."

"What do you mean?" she asks cautiously. Her expression gives way that she may not feel the same.

"Well, you seem to exude a lot more confidence lately, especially in the way you handle Chad."

"You're right. I do have a lot more confidence in dealing with him. You sharing your story has given me additional context to understanding how best to manage his personality. Maybe you're right." She says this as she sits up a little taller. "Maybe I do have a little more swagger."

I notice the empty glasses and bottle of wine, which prompts me to ask, "Why don't you all stay the night? The kids' bedroom is still set up downstairs. You can stay in the guest room. I'll get you a pair of pajamas."

"I don't know," Elsa says a little uneasily.

"C'mon, Mom! Let's stay! Can we, please?" Taylor pleads.

"Okay, we can stay," she says, still a little reluctant.

They stay the night, and we have a quick "fancy breakfast" in the morning before they leave and I jet off to spend the holiday season in Palm Springs.

It's been a little over a month, and I think I'm doing pretty well emotionally. I have my moments, but I'm feeling stronger and more stable. I can say "we broke up" without bursting into tears when someone asks about Chad and me.

I arrive at the airport, and I'm standing in line to check my bag. The weight of the situation hits me like a ton of bricks. I'm here *alone*. It was supposed to be our little foursome in that line. I'm not supposed to be standing here by myself.

I have a full life with friends, family, work, coworkers, and my dogs. Even when I spend time by myself, I love being alone. I've never truly felt lonely; until right now. And then tears start to well in my eyes. I've never been a crier. *What the hell is happening?* But once I do start, it's tough to stop. I'm at least able to pull myself together for the check-in process.

On the plane, the middle seat where Chad's supposed to sit is open. I notice the guy in the aisle seat keeps watching the front of the plane to see if anyone else is coming. I know that feeling of thinking, *Please, no one else get on the plane and sit in this seat.* He leans over as the plane is getting close to capacity, and they're announcing the boarding door will be closing soon and says, "Fingers crossed that this seat stays open."

"It will," I say confidently.

"How can you be so sure?"

"I bought that ticket, and the person that was supposed to be sitting there won't be coming."

"Oh really? Why not?" He asks with genuine curiosity.

As I begin to tell him, the tears that started welling up in my eyes back at the bag check line start to run down my face. *Thankfully I grabbed those tissues.*

"I'm sorry," I apologize for crying. While I don't want to let Chad be the source of my tears, I'm grieving the loss of my little family.

My seatmate introduces himself, "You do not need to apologize. I can imagine the holidays would be a hard time to go through a split. I'm Gregg, by the way. With two G's." He reaches over to shake my hand.

"So G-R-E-G?" I ask.

"No, G-R-E-G-G."

"Oh, so Gregg with three G's then?"

We share a chuckle, and Gregg with three G's helps get me through the rest of the flight. Well, Gregg and the three proseccos.

A
NEW
YEAR

TAYLOR'S AT MY HOUSE for a belated birthday celebration in early January. Over dinner, Taylor says, "The weirdest thing happened last winter, Ginny. We had to stop at Dad's apartment on the way to school to pick up a hockey stick."

I continue to listen attentively. I have a feeling this is going to be good.

"Mom waited in the car while Logan and I went into the apartment. When we walked in, we heard someone run up the stairs to Dad's bedroom."

"Oh? Who was it?"

"I don't know. But we ran up there and saw a girl in his bed. She threw the covers over herself completely. We both ran back down the stairs and ran to the patio door where we could see Mom in the car. We were waving at her and pointing up toward

Dad's bedroom and trying to tell her that someone was in there. She couldn't tell what was going on, so she just yelled for us and motioned to get out to the car right away."

I say, "Wow, that's quite a story."

"It's not a story. It's true, Ginny."

I just say, "Oh no, I didn't mean it like you were telling a story. I believe you." A brief look of confusion crosses Taylor's face, and we move on.

When I drop Taylor off, Elsa and I stand in her entryway, and I retell the story that Taylor shared.

She says, "Oh my gosh, yes. I remember that incident very well! I even confronted Chad about it because I'd already met you. When I inquired, he said, 'A group of us went to a concert and met at my place. She forgot her purse there and went back to get it.'"

Elsa continues, "I told him, 'Chad, I really like Ginny. And I like her for our kids.' He reassured me that he'd changed. I just said, 'Chad, don't mess this one up.'"

It doesn't appear Chad took Elsa's advice to heart.

I need to do a little shopping for my upcoming annual national sales meeting. Karen comes with me to my favorite little boutique. When we walk in, the owner comes out to greet us.

Oh no, she has that look on her face. Not that look. Please don't look at me with pity like that.

Then she looks at me with big eyes and says, "What *happened* to you? I mean, I know what happened to you, but what happened to the rest of you?"

One of the sales clerks comes out of the back and starts walking to me with arms spread wide to hug me. *Oh God, there's that look again.*

She says to me, "I was getting my hair done the other day, and my stylist told me he did the exact same thing to her friend!"

I know who she's referring to. The fury sets in. I'm still having a hard time managing my emotions through this grief process. There are flickers of anger through the hurt and pain.

How does her hairstylist, someone who's not in my circle, even know about my situation?

Why are they gossiping about me?

I gain my composure the best I can and say, "I feel terrible that she was victimized by him. I really do. But the situation isn't exactly the same. He didn't live with her. She didn't parent his children."

"I totally get that now that you say that."

"And I just have to ask that you please not talk about my situation with other people. When you discuss my personal details with anyone besides me, it simply becomes gossip. Please try to understand that this is very sensitive, especially because there are children involved."

Is my story that interesting? Why are people talking about me and my situation?

This journey has allowed me to feel the shame and humiliation of other people talking about me. This has opened my eyes to the idea that this happens more than we think. As a result, I've become more sensitive to sharing other people's personal information or stories, even when asked. I find myself often using the phrase, "It's not my story to tell."

I put this aside and start shopping. I step into the fitting room and start scanning through the items that are hanging across the rod. The clothes they've pulled for me and put in my fitting room are two and three sizes smaller than what I'm used to purchasing.

These are never going to fit.

To my surprise, they do. While people may be telling me I look great, I've never felt worse on the inside. This is an important reminder that just because someone is wearing it well doesn't mean it's comfortable.

Next up in the preparation process is my hair. I'm sitting in the chair getting reacquainted with my hairstylist from some years ago, doing the whole consultation thing. I'm staring at myself in the mirror under the horrible salon lighting. I explain to my old/new stylist, "I don't know what's going on. I feel like my hair is thinning. Look at this!" I say as I grab and hold a handful of my hair in my hand.

He starts taking a deeper look at my hair, standing over me, and asks with a hip thrust and a wrinkled nose, "Were you under a lot of stress recently?"

He knows nothing about me going through a breakup, let alone being in a relationship in the first place.

Wide-eyed, in the mirror, my eyes darting between him and me, I say, "I guess you could say something like that."

He points out, "You have an entire layer of hair that's about an inch long. That's about two months' growth."

I'm amazed at how my body has responded. But I know he's right and that our bodies know what's going on sometimes before our minds or hearts have the opportunity to catch up.

This must have been like when I got shingles. My body was sending me all of the signals. My body knew before my mind and my heart did.

RECENTLY
PLAYED

IT'S A BLUSTERY, COLD SATURDAY EVENING around 6:30 p.m. I'm driving downtown to meet my friend, Samantha, for dinner. There's a new restaurant we've been wanting to check out. I see Chad's car buzzing by me in the left lane heading towards downtown Minneapolis, where he's been living since I kicked him out.

Immediately, I have a visceral reaction. My heart starts racing. I feel my face turning red and hot, and my hands and body start shaking.

My first thought is, *Where are the kids? Saturday is supposed to be his night with his kids.* I've learned from Elsa that he doesn't keep his custody schedule very well. There's a family joke on her side that it's always "seminar season" for the nutrition company, and that's why he can't spend time with Taylor and Logan.

I'm just approaching the exit that I need to take. I speed up a bit to see into his brown coupe, and to my relief, the kids are there. There's Taylor's blonde-mopped head, sitting in the front seat, and Logan bundled up in the back seat.

Samantha's a few minutes late, and I'm still flustered when she arrives. I already ordered a glass of wine and told the server to keep 'em coming. I fill Samantha in on what just happened as she gets settled at the table.

Samantha looks deep in thought for a second and asks, "What would you say to him if you did see him?"

"I don't know. I haven't really thought about it. I'd like to think that I'd probably just try to ignore him."

Then I ask Samantha, "What would *you* say to him if you saw him?"

She quickly responds without hesitation, "Nothing. I wouldn't say anything to him. I would walk up to him and punch him in the face." And that is indicative of the kind of true friends that I have in my corner.

I'm preparing to go out on my first date post-split with Chad. It's been a few months now. It's a setup by Lauren. I don't feel ready for it, but I know I have to rip the bandage off at some point.

Thinking about tomorrow night's date, I'm taking a relaxing bath with pink Himalayan sea salts. I'm considering what to wear while sipping on a juicy glass of red wine. I'm fully in the zone, listening to music on my Sonos system when suddenly, I realize...

My Sonos system is still logged into Chad's account.

I haven't changed it. He uses the same account at home and at work. Typically, when you log in, you can select "Recently Played" and pick a station or playlist that you listen to frequently. This is how Chad utilizes his playlists at work.

I like to think that I can sometimes be an exemplary specimen of sophistication and maturity, but we all have our moments.

Once I get this in my head that I'm still logged into his account, I know that whatever I play on the account will show up as recently played for him as well. I could send him a message this way, which I think is genius.

So when Chad arrives to work the next morning, his "recently played" items will have songs like...

Imagine Dragons', "Bad Liar"

Post Malone's, "Psycho"

Demi Lovato's, "Mistake"

Katy Perry's, "The One That Got Away"

And Beck's classic, "Loser"

... to name a few.

BIRTHDAY

I'M LEANING AGAINST THE DOORWAY of Taylor and Logan's bedroom with my arms crossed. Each time I walk in here, it becomes more difficult. The reality that this isn't my life any longer continues to set in. What if I do meet someone that I want to consider a relationship with? It could be an uncomfortable conversation of why I'm single with no kids, but I have a kids' bedroom in my house.

After expressing these feelings to Lauren, she's adamant that it's time to get rid of the kids' bedroom. I hesitantly reach out to Elsa to see if she would like the furniture. I know the kids still have bunk beds at her house. They love their beds at my house, but I don't want to offend her by making it feel like I'm giving her hand-me-downs.

She graciously accepts my offer, and we schedule a moving day in March.

James is kind enough to come help with the move, so we can use his pickup. Elsa brought her sister-in-law and her truck in the hopes that we can get everything moved in one trip.

The four of us load up both trucks. Elsa and her sister-in-law take off first, and I finish loading some of the smaller items while James is securing everything in the bed of his pickup truck. We're just minutes behind them.

As James pulls onto the highway, I yell "Oh my gosh, one of the mattresses just went flying out into the middle of the highway!" James has to pull off at the next exit, loop back around, and pull the truck over on the side of the road. With adrenaline pumping, we wait for a break in the cars flying by, run out into the road, grab the mattress, and run back across the highway before reloading it into the truck.

A police officer comes by to see if we need any help. We don't have enough bungee cords to secure everything, so we have to leave a piece of furniture on the side of the off-ramp and come back to get it on a second trip.

I'm relaxing on the couch, just having returned from a quick trip to celebrate my birthday in Tulum with Lauren. While scrolling and getting caught up on Instagram, I see Chad's first post since our split, about a 2.0 version of his business. I'm confident this is no coincidence that it's on my birthday.

I'm continuing the celebration by enjoying some cocktails, and I'm probably not using my best judgment when I comment on his post.

I remark, "Fantastic! So does this mean that you're no longer a fraud and can provide some stability for your children? Which means you won't live in six places in less than five years?" With a follow-up comment because I couldn't help myself, "Oh, and did that process server ever connect with you? I sure hope I gave them the right address! *fingers crossed emoji*" Not my proudest moment.

Shortly after I post this and take it down, I get a text message from Taylor's phone. The message appears to be written by Chad. It says, "Don't ever call my dad out again, especially on social media. Or else we are going to have problems."

Elsa, who I've become close with, recently made her Instagram private. This all feels orchestrated by Chad. I stopped hearing from Elsa and the kids. While it feels painful and as though the kids and Elsa have slipped through my fingertips and out of my life, I back off and allow some distance.

Did Chad somehow manage to flip the script on me and paint me as the villain?

SUMMER

A COUPLE OF MONTHS GO by with no communication from Elsa or the kids. My heart's heavy over this, but I respect that she may feel it's the best thing for them. Then, out of the blue, I get a FaceTime call from Logan. It's another one of those getting-the-wind-knocked-out-of-you moments.

My suitcase is open on the hotel room bed as I'm packing my bag to travel home from another work destination. I don't answer because I physically can't. I feel paralyzed looking at the phone in my hand and unable to touch the green answer button. I think maybe it's a mistake. But I know it isn't when it's followed up immediately with a text that says, "I miss you *heart emoji*"

After flying home, I'm out with Anne enjoying a glass of wine on a patio. My phone is on the table when it buzzes, and the next text rolls in from Logan. "I want to see you."

Another gut punch. Anne can sense something by the look on my face, "What's going on? Is everything ok?"

I turn the phone around and show her the message.

"Shut. *Up*," she says. "What are you going to do?"

I take a deep breath and say, "I feel like I need to respond. First I should check in with Elsa and make sure she's okay with me communicating with them."

I reply to Logan, "I miss you too! I would love to see you."

"Right now. I want to see you right now."

Anne and I chuckle at the innocence of that message.

"I'd love to see you right now, but I can't. I'll check with your mom to see if we can plan something soon."

I reach out to Elsa, a little nervous about how she'll respond, but she's open and agreeable. So we plan a time for me and Logan to get together and also a girls' night out for the two of us.

I pick Logan up from school. I turn to the backseat and ask, "So what would you like to do?!"

"Let's go to your house. I want to see Emilio!"

My heart drops into my stomach. Before I can say anything, the look on my face gives it away. I can see the tears welling up. "Oh, Sweetheart."

"No!"

"I'm so sorry. Yes, Emilio passed away."

"Why does every animal I love have to die? When did he die?"

"Last month." I can see Logan is trying to resist crying, and I want to make sure I make it known that it's okay to express sadness. "Do you feel like crying?"

I see the little head nodding up and down in the back seat. No words are spoken, but it becomes clear that giving permission to cry is exactly what was needed at that moment.

So with a little encouragement, I reach my hand back so we can hold hands and say, "It's okay to cry. I've cried a lot over losing Emilio. He was such a good little buddy."

"I know. He's the best! I miss him."

"Me too. Do you still want to go to my house? We could go see Francine."

"Yeah."

The soft glow of the lights begin to shine a little brighter. As the music starts to fade overhead, the sounds of the clanking dishes in the kitchen become more apparent. Elsa and I both become aware that the staff is beginning to gather at the bar as their shifts are ending. This prompts me to look at my watch and say, "Oh my gosh. We've been here for almost four hours!"

Time tends to fly by when Elsa and I get together.

"Oh geez. Yeah, we better get going. I'm so glad we caught up. I feel terrible that you thought that we didn't want to see you." Elsa replies.

"Well, I wasn't sure. I got that message from Taylor, and then you made your Instagram private. I hadn't heard anything, and I wanted to be respectful. I thought maybe you just thought it was for the best." I shrugged.

"And I totally thought you met someone and that it might be weird for you to have a relationship with the kids," she says, shaking her head slowly at the misunderstanding.

"No. Never. I'll always have room for them in my life. When I do meet someone, they're just going to have to accept the kids being a part of my world."

Lou and I are walking to a local French restaurant a few blocks from her house for dinner. It's a gorgeous Minnesota summer night. The full trees are blowing in the soft breeze, making the evening temperature comfortable as we walk side by side on the sidewalk.

She informs me that a friend of hers will be joining us for dinner. I've met her a few times.

As we're enjoying a glass of wine and our appetizers, Lou and I notice another client of Chad's, Maya, a couple of tables down from ours. When she sees us, she beams and comes running over. We all greet one another with big hugs.

"Oh my gosh! I have missed you two so much! Where have you been?" Maya asks.

Lou jumps right in, "Chad cheated on Ginny. We started going to another gym. You should join us!"

I add, "Well, that's just one part of the story. It's all kind of disturbing, actually."

Maya looks curious. "I've wondered what's been going on. Things have seemed so weird with him. He cancels all of the time! He never seems to have or talk about his kids anymore. If I knew more about the story, would I still want to go there?"

Lou quickly says, "No. You sure wouldn't. Ginny's being polite. It's very upsetting."

I add, "It would certainly be up to you. No judgment."

Maya asks me, "Would you be willing to sit down and have coffee with me?"

"Of course! Any time," I say.

"Okay, I'll text you and we'll get something scheduled. It was so good to see you two! Enjoy your dinner. Ginny, I'll see you soon." And Maya goes back to join her group at her table.

As we sit back down, Lou's friend looks at her and says, "Don't disparage Chad, Lou. You need to stop disparaging him."

Lou and I exchange a look, and it's my turn to jump in. "Lou didn't say anything that wasn't the truth. People deserve to know the truth if they ask questions. They can make their own decisions from the facts. And if you find the truth disparaging, then that probably speaks to your view of the monstrosity of his actions."

On the walk home with Lou, I express, "It kind of bothers me when you say that Chad cheated on me."

"Well, he did!"

"Yes, he did. But that was the tip of the iceberg. There is so much more involved in the situation. It almost feels like it minimizes the circumstances for me. Does that make sense?"

Lou understandingly replies, "Yes, that does make sense. I'm really sorry I never thought about it from that perspective, and I really appreciate you sharing that with me."

I get in my car to drive home and as I pull away from Lou's house, I'm overcome with a sense of gratitude for the important friend that she's become in my life. I remember after meeting her and Anne early on and thinking they're my people. Turns out, they really are.

I'm at another work meeting in Huntington Beach. It's the same hotel I brought Chad and the kids to last summer for our family "field trip." Upon arrival, I head up to the rooftop to grab lunch by myself. As I sit there in the salt-scented breeze, I look down at the miles and miles of white sand beach against the blue sky and watch the waves crashing ashore.

My emotions are running rampant, and the tears well up in my eyes behind my sunglasses. I can almost picture Taylor and Logan running into the ocean for the first time last year.

I text Sara and ask, "Can you talk?" Like a true friend, she calls me back right away to talk through what I'm feeling.

"What's going on? Is everything okay?" she asks, concerned.

"Oh yes. I'm just sitting here crying on the rooftop in the restaurant at the hotel in Huntington Beach. I was here with Chad and the kids this same time last year. It's just making me so sad."

"Oh, Ginny. I'm so sorry. I bet it does."

"It's kind of embarrasing that I'm still crying over it. People are probably wondering what the hell is wrong with this woman sitting here by herself with tears rolling down her face," I say the last part with a half chuckle.

"You should not be embarrassed whatsoever. I'm sure being there is stirring up a lot of emotion. I wish I could give you a big hug right now."

"Thanks, Sara."

These feelings of sadness are all part of my process. What dawns on me as I sit watching the people and families frolicking about the beach is that I want what they have.

I'm grieving and processing loss. While we often think about grief being associated with losing someone through death, grief can be brought on by the loss of people still living.

Grieving and loss come in many shapes and sizes. For me, I'm still healing from the loss of the life I had created. I'd changed nearly everything about my day-to-day life to embrace having and building this family of four. I believed that was my future. And now it's gone.

Everyone's path is different, and their grief will have its own unique journey and timeline. Cherishing and celebrating these big moments I was able to experience by being a part of these kids' lives is part of my healing process.

OPEN
MIND

I'M IN THE CAR ON A RIDE-ALONG with a sales rep in the San Francisco Bay area when I get an invite to a women's retreat in Mexico. It piques my interest. I say under my breath not realizing it's loud enough for the rep to hear, "Where the hell is San Miguel de Allende?"

The sales rep gasps, reaches across the car console to put her hand on my arm, turns squarely to me, and says, "That is one of my favorite places on earth. I don't know why you are bringing it up, but if you have the opportunity to go, you have to go! It's amazing!"

The retreat is focused on nutrition and meditation. I've never slowed down to meditate for one single minute before in my life.

I do yoga; is that similar enough?

A few years ago, I may have dismissed this type of retreat and said something like, "You all go on with your hippie-dippy selves and have a blast." But something is pulling me toward it. I feel like I need this for myself. Both inside and out.

I say, "I don't know what I'm getting myself into, but I'm going to go into this with an open mind." I had no idea how momentous this would be. I'll embark on this adventure in November, almost exactly one year post-split.

Later in the week, I received another message from a recruiter at a company that's been contacting me about various positions since January. For nine months, I've ignored every single one of them. Having been with my company for over eight years, I haven't contemplated making a job change.

This time is different. My mind is open. Something sparks my interest, and I start connecting some dots to people I know working there. As I begin the interview process, everything seems to be aligning perfectly to this new, more open version of myself.

I love the authenticity and "no ego" style of the people I meet along the way. The product and vision of the company are exciting. I know it's something I want to be a part of. I received the job offer the night before I left for the retreat in November and gladly accepted.

In preparation for the retreat, I'm out running some errands. I walk into a coffee shop that I frequent. I order my coffee to go. As I wait for my latte and take in my surroundings, I notice an attractive man. And then I notice another one. It doesn't register at the moment.

I walk out to my car and put my latte in the cupholder. I start the car, put my seatbelt on, and get settled.

Holy shit. I just found a man attractive. I just found TWO men attractive! I'm not dead inside. Hallelujah!

Chad made me so turned off to men, that I realized I hadn't been able to find a man attractive for almost a year. Seeing this shift in myself, makes me do a little happy dance in my car.

RETREAT

IT'S ON THE RETREAT WHERE I MEDITATE for the first time. The meditation is guided and focuses on inner child work. Deep shit.

This is the catalyst to where true growth begins for me. There is no timeline for grief. I've worked through the anger and sadness stages. Now it's time for the acceptance stage—the healing.

Many people turn to traditional therapy or their faith during difficult times. I've gone to therapy before, and I think it's great. However, getting introduced to meditation really resonates with me.

Turning to meditation and looking within myself becomes a significant part of my healing journey. There's no one right way, but this is what works for me. When I look inside, I'm taken back to a childhood memory from when I was four years old.

I've always known that I cut my golden ringlets off as a little girl. What's fascinating is that I remember doing it. It's one of, if not my first, vivid childhood memories.

At four years old, I stood on a step stool in my parent's bathroom at the black sink over the yellow carpet and picked up a small pair of scissors. I grabbed as much hair as I could gather in my little hand and gripped the scissors with the other. I cut the lock of hair all the way down to the root. I never understood why—until now.

I had a one-on-one session afterwards to debrief with the meditation guide.

She began by asking, "Were you able to connect with your younger self?"

"Yeah, I was," I say. Still in a bit of disbelief at the vividness of the visualization.

"What did you experience tapping into your inner child during the meditation?"

I explain to her the details of what I remember and follow up with some additional context, "My mom was in an inpatient treatment facility for addiction. My dad was working like crazy to make sure the family was taken care of. My sister was sixteen at the time, and she was trying to manage high school, sports, taking care of me and James, and attempting to have a social life. Everyone was spread thin and exhausted. My sister was supposed to be watching me, but she fell asleep on the couch because she was so run down. At that moment, I proclaimed that I was a big girl and could take care of myself. So, I cut my hair."

I pause for a moment to absorb this.

I continue, "When we visited my mom in treatment, she cried when she saw me. She was heartbroken that my beautiful hair was gone and my appearance was altered."

I reflect for a moment about this reaction. It brings to light the importance of appearances and what people think of you. This is where the emotion of shame, perfectionism, and living through ego come into play. I was taught to care and prioritize what everyone else thinks of me. I was so worried about what people thought my whole life that I was always fearful of making a mistake or disappointing people.

Meditating and being brought back to this moment, I now understand that I became an independent adult at four years old. It helps me understand why I am who I am.

The meditation guide chimes in, "It's no wonder people have always used phrases like, 'you're an old soul' to describe you. You weren't allowed to experience and express emotion as a child because you had to become an adult as a four-year-old."

With this new information, I came to a deeper understanding that the adults around me modeled behavior where you don't express or discuss your emotions outwardly. Disagreements are perceived as negative, brushed under the rug, and never spoken of again.

My understanding of being a grown-up means stifling your feelings and being tough, hence my nickname *M & M*. Understanding this as a thirty-nine-year-old woman, I begin the journey to healing my inner child and discovering my heart. This includes processing and expressing emotion and grief in a healthy manner.

After returning home from the retreat, meditation becomes a part of my regular routine. Many more aha moments continue to occur after the trip. Meditation has helped me dig deep into understanding my own patterns and my familial patterns and how that has played into what I have allowed into my life. Knowing that much of this is stemmed from what's familiar to me.

This is also where I truly start to embrace and trust my intuition. How did I miss so many red flags with Chad? I didn't miss them—I merely didn't trust myself enough, so I ignored them. All of those feelings—a punch in the gut, a wave rushing over me, or my hands turning tingly or numb—were all the signals that I didn't believe in myself enough to acknowledge during my relationship with Chad.

I now know to trust myself and realize that I know the answers. I don't have to seek them outside of myself or seek validation for what I know to be true. Through looking into myself, I've relearned trust. I've regained the trust in myself to know that I have the truth.

I've learned that meditation doesn't always have to be as intense as digging into your inner child. Meditating for shorter periods, even a minute or two, can make a tremendous impact on how I respond—or don't—to situations.

I may sit in my car, close my eyes and breathe in for a count of four and out for a count of four. I might do this after being cut off in a traffic situation or being treated like shit in the grocery store. This is easily done in the parking lot before getting out of my car or driving. It helps to bring a sense of calm and avoid reflecting the treatment I just received onto someone else.

CRABS

I STARTED TO PAY MORE ATTENTION to my relationships and the energy they deposit or withdraw from my life. I began to check in with my emotional bank account after each interaction. You don't need to leave every encounter feeling like you got a huge deposit, but it's important to recognize patterns. If you feel depleted after every interaction with someone, it makes sense to evaluate the investment into the relationship because life is short. It's feasible you realize your value and they haven't yet.

I'm getting a facial from my long-time esthetician - and sometimes therapist. She's an intuitive and mindful individual whom I often seek perspective and insight from.

I explain to her, "I've had a couple of bizarre interactions lately—interactions that stand out because they're quite opposite of all of the other experiences I've grown accustomed to more recently with people being vulnerable and warm."

After sharing the details, she says with certainty, "That's the crab mentality."

"What's the crab mentality?" I ask.

"You've never heard of the crab phenomenon?" she asks, pulling her head back.

"No! Now I need to know more about it. Enlighten me." I say, eager to learn.

"Well, if you put crabs in a bucket and one tries to escape, the other crabs try to pull that one back down instead of trying to lift one another up and help them escape."

"Oh wow. So what you're saying is this sadly happens with humans as well?"

"Yeah, when you're working on yourself and growing, seeing this new version of you can make others uncomfortable. Instead of supporting you, they may awkwardly attempt to tear you down with words or actions."

This is a big revelation for someone like me; someone who always tries to see the good in people. My dad's always said I live life through rose-colored glasses. I always thought it was an insult – until now.

It exposes the concept that perhaps watching someone grow and evolve amplifies seeing things in themselves that they aren't quite ready to address. Everyone around you has the choice to grow with you or stay stagnant. This is a helpful reminder that if others around you aren't growing, even if it feels like they are trying to pull you back down rather than lift you up, stay the course. If you leave a few crabs behind, you will gain something remarkable by accomplishing your goals.

Humans naturally tend to hold on to this hope that relationships, especially romantic ones, are indestructible. We don't seem to think about the end of them. Instead, we dream about their future and believe they will be what carries us through life. In contrast, we know that death is inevitable. Whether it's expected or not, it's never easy.

We anticipate and expect to be sad and grieve death. And society tells us that's okay. On the flip side, there isn't a rule book for us to follow to grieve other types of trauma and grief, like the end of a relationship.

That may be why the end of my relationship with Chad shook me to my core. There seemed to be this unspoken expectation that I'd be strong and power through it.

The end of my relationship with Chad turned out to be a blessing in many ways. And there were some very surprising and valuable things that I learned throughout my relationship with him.

I learned about butt wipes. I'd never used them regularly before. But now they're in every bathroom.

I also learned how to neatly tie electric cords. This is an important skill that I will carry throughout the rest of my life.

There are no ifs, ands, or buttwipes about it. I've been able to take one of the most devastating experiences of my life and turn it into some of the best learnings to incorporate personal growth and overall wellness into my journey.

One of the greatest gifts I've been given in this process was the experience of parenting. Some people, especially moms, may balk at the idea of me labeling myself a parent. I was invested. I was present. I was a parent. I provided love and care. It was a wonderful learning experience.

Elsa and I continue with what we call our modern little family. We want to set an example that people and relationships aren't disposable. This was an important connection I made through learning about myself and my familial patterns. I grew up in a family where if you have a fight with someone, you cut them out of your life. Both of my parents had these patterns in their families.

And not surprisingly, the same behavior was modeled among my siblings as well. While I don't have children of my own, this is an opportunity for me to help break that pattern with two impressionable kids that are learning the importance and value of relationships and people.

As part of our modern family routine, Elsa and I have regular girls' nights. We also consistently plan time to get together as a foursome. Whether it's dinner or going for a bike ride, we carve out quality time.

Elsa and the kids invited me over for dinner. And at the kids' request, I pick up everyone's takeout orders from their favorite Asian restaurant by my house. We used to order it often when they lived with me.

As the four of us are chatting over dinner, Elsa says to the kids, "So, tell Ginny about your new puppy." She looks at them and then looks at me.

"Oh yeah! We got a puppy at our dad's."

I'm doing my best to keep my composure and not choke on my food. I'm horrified. *The dog abuser got a puppy.*

Elsa says, "Tell her what kind of dog it is." She shoots me another look.

"Oh, it's a Cavalier King Charles Spaniel," Taylor said.

I swallow hard.

Elsa says, "And tell Ginny what color it is."

This time I shot her a look, like, *Oh, hell naw.*

Logan proudly chimes in, "Red like Francine!" and jumps up to show me a photo displayed on the phone.

The kids go downstairs after dinner to play. They aren't at the bottom of the staircase before I say to Elsa in a hushed tone,

"What kind of psychopath would get the same type and color of dog as me?"

"I know! I couldn't believe it. It's so weird."

"And how did he even afford it? I mean, considering he doesn't even keep up on his payments to you."

"Well, supposedly the first one he got had a heart condition and died, so he said this one was basically free. It doesn't make any sense to me since he would have had to pay for the first one."

"Wow, that poor dog. That seriously breaks my heart."

"I know. It's really sad. In other alarming news, Chad recently got Taylor and Logan new phones. When I opened Logan's phone, I noticed that they were all linked to Chad's cloud. There were at least five apps in there that were for threesomes, swingers, or last-minute hook-ups. I'm so grateful that they weren't the ones to discover it!"

It's difficult, while not surprising, to hear of Chad's continued pernicious ways. It's beautiful to see that Elsa, despite an uphill battle, persists to ensure that his patterns and behaviors don't get transferred onto Logan and Taylor.

A father earns the opportunity to be a dad—to be the guy that instills and shapes the kind of young people he releases into the world. Many do not get lucky in that department. Fortunately, I sure did.

HALLMARK
HOLIDAY

I WAKE UP AND GIVE FRANCINE a few pets before rolling over to check the time on my phone. It's Sunday, February 14, 2021. Immediately, I notice I have several missed calls and text messages in the middle of the night from both James and my mom. Considering I've had little to no communication with either of them recently, I draw in a quick gasp.

Fuck… my dad.

I skip the slow wake-up routine Francine and I have established and shoot out of bed as I dial my mom. No answer.

I call James as I walk out to the living room. He picks up and, in a soft and deflated tone, says, "Hey."

"I saw I had missed calls from you and Mom. Is it Dad? Is he okay?"

"I'm so sorry, Ginny."

"What?!"

"He's gone."

"No!"

"Yeah. I've been dreading talking to you."

"No. No, no, no, no, no, no, no." I can't breathe, and I sink to the floor, grasping my chest. "What happened?" I manage.

"He had a heart attack."

"Oh, God. Hopefully he didn't suffer."

"I don't think he suffered for too long."

"That's at least a little comforting to hear. Are you in town?"

"No, I'm in California."

"When are you coming back? We're going to have to put together a funeral."

"I know. I don't know when I'll be back yet. I'll keep you posted."

"Ok, thanks. I need to go try to process all of this. I'll call you later."

I hang up and think, *My dad died of a heart attack on Valentine's Day? Oh, how cliche, Dad. I can only imagine how you are chuckling about this one.*

The irony for me is that Valentine's Day will never be the same. It's never had any real significance in my life, but now it will have true sentiment.

My mom calls me back. I listen as she tells me her version of the details of what happened. Next, I offer to come over to her house. I'm immediately put to work upon arrival. First, I have to call the funeral home. Then, I have to call the hospital to arrange for his body to be picked up.

The funeral director calls me back to tell me he's having trouble getting the hospital to release his body. So I have to call the hospital a second time to arrange for his body to be picked up.

We schedule a time to go to the funeral home tomorrow to make the arrangements for his service and burial. That's when we'll pick out the casket and flower arrangements.

I pour myself a glass of heart-healthy red wine and sit down on the couch when I get home later than I would've liked that night. I need to get to work on writing and creating the program; picking the songs that will be played, the readings, and who will read the readings; and writing the obituary for the newspaper and the eulogy that my mom instructed me I'll be delivering.

I'm put in a position to take the lead. I somehow need to get through the week and the service. It feels like there's a lot on my shoulders.

On Friday morning, I wake up and know I need to pull off a celebration of my dad's life that will honor him and make him proud.

I'm the first to arrive at the funeral home. I find the funeral director and ask, "Can we turn off this depressing music? I made a playlist of oldies music in honor of my dad. It would be really cool if we could play that instead during the viewing." My dad and I spent uncountable hours listening to the oldies together; it's where I got my love of music.

"Yes, that would be great! You wouldn't believe how tired of this music we get," he replies.

Once we get the music situation handled, I step into the still of the quiet room and have my last moments alone with my dad's physical body before family and guests start to arrive.

During the eulogy, I take pride in honoring my biggest fan, my hero, and the greatest influence in my life. The man who will forever be the standard in which I measure all men.

Through the tears, I share many of my dad's accomplishments, some of his favorite stories, and some of his famous dad-isms, like "You made your bed, now you have to sleep in it," and his most famous quote, "You are the architect of your own destiny."

It's Sunday. I'm back at my mom's house to write and send all of her thank you notes to everyone that attended my dad's service and sent condolences.

As we stand in her entryway, she grabs me by the shoulders and says, "I don't care what anyone says, I think you did a good job."

"What do you mean?"

"Oh, you know."

"No, I don't know. Who said I didn't do a good job?"

"Well, James and Karen had their fair share of things to say."

"Well, truthfully, it doesn't matter what they think. It was for Dad, and I know that he would have been proud of how he was honored."

This sort of exchange is typical with my family. A conversation like this between my mom and my younger self would have been damaging for me. Now that I've healed past patterns, I can see beyond his manipulation and see it for its face value. The younger version of me would have gotten caught up in this drama, but I no longer get roped into abusive behavior and treatment.

The growing version of me—growing, not grown, because our work is never done—would have worried about what everyone else thought. That's living through ego, like when I would get upset about people viewing me as a victim after splitting up with Chad. Now I live through my heart and know my truth. I can protect my peace.

PRETTY
SNOWFLAKE

DR. MASARU EMOTO, a Japanese scientist, studied the effect of human sounds, thoughts, words, and intentions on the formation of snowflakes. It turns out, water that's exposed to loving and compassionate human intention forms aesthetically pleasing crystal formations, i.e., snowflakes.

In contrast, he found that water met with fearful and discordant human intention results in disfigured and disconnected-looking snowflakes.

This begs the question; If humans are composed mostly of water, what happens when we start talking to and treating others and ourselves as beautiful snowflakes?

Upon leaving the retreat in Mexico, we were tasked with creating positive intentions for ourselves. Each attendee created five of them during the trip, including me. While we were completing the activity, I thought, *why haven't I been treating and talking to myself like I would a cute puppy?*

It makes sense to surround yourself with others that treat you with positive and loving intentions. It's just as powerful in a positive manner as in a negative manner. I've never really thought about speaking to and treating myself this way. It's time to start.

Over coffee with Lou, she asks, "How long has it been since you broke up with Chad?"

"It's been almost exactly three years."

Since then, I've changed jobs, my relationships with family and friends have evolved— some have run their course and some have strengthened—but, most importantly, I've evolved.

She leans forward in her chair and says, "Wow. I can't believe it's been that long already! But it also feels like I've known you forever."

"It does seem like a lifetime ago and also like yesterday sometimes. What's interesting is that as I reflect on going through all of the emotions of grief, including anger—*especially* anger…" I'm saying in a self-deprecating tone, when Lou interrupts with a laugh.

I join her in sharing that laugh before finishing my thought…

"That angry feeling really does feel like a lifetime ago. I can now express gratitude for what I went through. I wouldn't be where I am today if it weren't for this experience. I probably wouldn't have my current job. I definitely wouldn't have you or Anne as close friends. And I certainly wouldn't have Elsa and the kids in my life in the capacity that I do."

"That's all true. How do you think you got through it all?"

"A lot of wine."

Lou gives a hearty chuckle knowing I'm making light of it. We clink our coffee mugs together.

I continue, "That's a great question. I've put a lot of thought into this."

I get lost in thought for a moment as I feel the warmth from my coffee mug with both hands wrapped around it. I glance at my left ringless finger and smile. There was a time I thought there was a possibility that I would marry him—a thought I can't begin to fathom now. The absence of a ring feels empowering and I'm reminded of how much I've grown and shifted.

I come back to the moment and share, "I think what got me through everything was sort of what I've boiled down into this three-ingredient recipe. I continually practice curiosity, I use daily positive intentions, and I emphasize nurturing myself."

"Yeah, I think I need to start doing more with positive intentions. You gave me a beautiful affirmation last year. I used it with my mala beads. I remember feeling great after repeating that affirmation 108 times."

We pause for a sip of coffee. I can see Lou get lost in thought for a moment and imagine her wheels turning about what positive intentions she might want to start integrating into her daily routine.

I continue, "I couldn't have done any of this without a lot of support from some pretty amazing people in my corner. What's heartening is that I recognize the people I've allowed into my life in recent years are warm, vulnerable, authentic, accepting and loving—like you."

"Well, that's because that's reflective of you."

I lean in, "That's so kind of you to say. It's not to say that some of my longer standing relationships don't have this, too, but I truly feel like there's been an overwhelming shift. I now see that this is the type of energy and light I welcome and attract into my life.

And as I've removed toxic and abusive behaviors and patterns there is a spotlight on them when I do encounter them now. It's almost as though someone handed me a magnifying glass over the past few years and now these behaviors are amplified. Things are much more clear to me now."

"You've been through a lot and you've done a lot of hard work. It's been really fun to see and wonderful to be a part of."

One of Lou's friends walks in and stops to say hello. After they greet each other, she says, "I hope I'm not interrupting anything."

"Not at all. Please join us." To fill her in on what we're talking about, I give her as brief of a synopsis as possible of my story. She leans over the table towards me and replies, "Can I share my story really quickly with you?"

Forty-five minutes later, she's finishing her story across from me with tears streaming down her cheeks. Her trauma is from over twenty-five years ago and it's clear she hasn't yet healed from it. Perhaps this is her opportunity to start. I'm handing her tissues and am honored that she felt comfortable enough to share her trauma with me.

She finishes by saying, "Thank you for sharing your story and creating an environment to make me feel comfortable to be vulnerable and share mine."

As I sit across from Lou and her friend, I reflect on how much my life has improved and interactions with people have changed. I'm grateful for the path that's been chosen for me and the path I chose. Growth can be uncomfortable and it can be difficult to leave what is familiar to us, even if it means leaving existing in an abusive and toxic frequency.

Everyone experiences trauma, heartbreak, adversity, or disappointment in some capacity. Through these traumatic and painful experiences, we all have the power within ourselves to decide how we come out on the other side of them—we are the architects of our own destiny after all. It's also unnecessary to wait for a traumatic experience to begin working on ourselves. I only wish someone had told me that long ago.

METAMORPHOSIS

MY TRANSFORMATION SLOWLY STARTED after a traumatic experience about six months before I met Chad. It began when my brother passed away in February 2017. It was incredibly painful. I was assigned the responsibility to call and tell my parents.

As the baby of the family, I've always been the peacemaker—a people pleaser. I always want harmony and for everyone to be happy. That can be a lot to shoulder, but this felt like an almost unconquerable task ahead of me. I had to call my dad, the pillar of strength that I admired and saw so much of in myself, and tell him that his son was gone. I knew I was about to shatter his heart.

Even though I've heard the announcement countless times on an airplane, "Place the oxygen mask over your own nose and mouth before assisting others," I hadn't yet fully absorbed the idea that if you run out of oxygen, you won't be able to help anyone else. You have to care for yourself before you can truly care for anyone else.

I'd never been one to express my feelings and I almost felt

ashamed at how I couldn't control them after losing my brother. His death was a complete shock. One of the most profound moments through that process was when I called my boss at the time to tell him. It was the day after we learned my brother was gone. I needed to get a hold of my boss to let him know that I wouldn't be working that week and why.

I sat at my kitchen island staring at my phone on the granite countertop. I planned to call my boss on the speaker because I was shaking uncontrollably, so much so that I couldn't hold on to the phone. The eerie quiet in the house resembled the void in my head. I couldn't seem to muster the words that I needed to say.

As I sat on the gray leather barstool, I finally gathered the courage to call my boss.

When he answered and I told him the news, he said, "Oh Ginny…I am so sorry!" He cried with me on the other end of the phone. I can still hear the words and the sound of him crying like it was yesterday.

It felt like I was being given permission to express my emotions without judgment, and I will never forget that feeling. I always look back at it with immense gratitude. This made me start to get curious and chip away at that thin, outer coating to allow the softer side of me to become exposed.

With the outer coating being cracked open, in some ways I attribute this as a small fragment of why I allowed Chad into my life. And more so, why I opened my heart to Taylor and Logan.

The contrast of how I handled loss and grief then as compared to how I can handle it now is vastly different. I'm more equipped now to manage my emotions and move through loss.

My curiosity led me to start reading and learning. If there's a book on healing yourself, attachment styles, family patterns, romantic relationships, or personality disorders, it's possible I've read it.

I learned the difference between narcissism, sociopaths, and psychopaths. These are terms thrown around flippantly, but I truly desired to understand the differences and where some of the characteristics interlace. Most importantly, I wanted to comprehend how I've been impacted by these behaviors and how to change that for myself and others moving forward.

Gaslighting, deflecting, projecting, and posturing are all techniques that I came to understand that I've experienced.

Elsa and I have shared many stories of our experiences with these techniques and how Taylor and Logan have even been exposed to them.

Elsa says to me over dinner, "So, I had to give Taylor a lesson on what gaslighting is the other day."

"Why? What happened?"

"Well, Taylor heard Chad with a girl in his bedroom. Chad denied it. Taylor is insistent on knowing what the noises were coming from Chad's bedroom. Taylor asked when Chad denied it, 'Why is he making me feel like I'm crazy?' So, I explained… that's what gaslighting is."

I encountered gaslighting when Chad attempted to make me question how his two erectile dysfunction pills disappeared after we got back from Italy. This technique is meant to make you feel like you're crazy and begin to doubt reality. This was incredibly effective because I was already feeling insecure and crazy for counting his pills in the first place. Rather than having the confidence to trust my intuition that I was doing this for a reason, he was able to capitalize on my insecurity.

Chad's a master deflector, too. He was deflecting when he said he couldn't be blamed if the security system wasn't working properly. He was trying to remove the blame from himself by shifting it to technology.

Projecting is when someone doesn't like something in themselves and calls out how much they despise it in others.

I'm not a doctor and have no credentials to make any diagnoses. From what I've been able to research, I've learned that this is quite common with narcissists. They may complain about how much attention someone needs, only because they desire the attention themselves. It's a mechanism used to shame others in order to elevate their own sense of self. Tearing others down is how they build themselves up. There is also an intense need for control for narcissists. It's common for them to try to alienate you from others and you may notice patterns of them always being *wronged* by people and dismissing people and relationships.

While these experiences weren't funny at the time, Elsa and I have also been able to ultimately share some deep belly laughs over some of Chad's posturing.

"Oh my gosh, Ginny. Before we were married, Chad got me this fake Cartier watch. I was kind of embarrassed to wear it. It needed a new battery so I brought it to a big retail chain store. The girl at the jewelry counter said that she didn't think she could change the battery on an expensive watch like a CartieR … emphasis on the second R."

The way she is retelling the story makes us both laugh uncontrollably.

"I simply told her to go ahead and change the battery because it was indeed a CartieR."

I shared my posturing experience with her, "When I was buying my car and the salesman told us the payment amount, Chad responded, 'That's not that bad.'"

Elsa replied, "I don't even know how much the payment was, but I'm certain Chad could never have afforded whatever that amount was."

"Exactly! But he wanted to impress and mislead me into thinking he was financially sound."

The warning signs were all there. I was simply leaning into what was familiar to me. Now I can identify these learned behaviors and patterns and have a better understanding of how to navigate through them.

The doors part in front of me and I mind the gap as I step into the tram at the airport. As I board the tram, I notice a girl and assess that she's probably in her twenties. She's on the phone and she's crying hard. My heart hurts for her even though I have no idea who she is or why she might be crying.

A few years ago, I might not have given it a second thought. However, another passenger, a middle-aged man, must have noticed that I was paying attention to her. He gives me a glance that indicates, "Geez, what's the matter with her?" as he looks at her and then makes eye contact with me.

This doesn't sit well with me. It feels judgy and mean.

The girl sits down on the bench near the front window. I lean down to her and ask softly, "Are you okay?"

She's crying so hysterically that she can't speak, so she just shrugs her shoulders and nods her head a little.

"Is there anything I can do for you?" I ask, even though it seems likely there's nothing I'd be able to do for a stranger on a moving train at the airport. It appears like she could use a little compassion and understanding.

She shakes her head no and mouths, "Thank you."

I arrive at the hotel for the work conference I'm attending and see an industry colleague, Janet, walking across the hotel lobby.

She notices me and waves as she's walking across the room. I wave back from the table I'm sitting at in the grand lobby having a quick lunch. Janet and I've been in the same industry for over fifteen years and have followed similar career paths. She's someone I have tremendous respect for and I always enjoy an opportunity to connect with her.

She walks over. "I want to catch up with you! I need to run upstairs quickly, but will you be here for a few minutes?"

"I sure will."

True to her word, she comes strolling back over to my table from the elevators and takes a seat. "How *are* you?" she asks genuinely.

"I'm doing well, thank you. How have you been?"

"Oh I'm good. Just busy, you know. Okay, so last time we saw each other, we were sitting next to one another on a flight on the way to Orlando. You were in a serious relationship. Is that still going?"

"No, things didn't work out with that."

"Oh, I'm sorry to hear. You seemed so happy."

"Thank you. It's okay," I respond sincerely. And for the first time, I realize not only is it okay, but I am okay. I am better than okay. "Honestly, it was a pretty horrible experience, but I wouldn't change a thing. Actually, I don't think it happened *to* me, rather *for* me. Everything works out exactly how it is supposed to. I've learned so much about myself and life through the process."

"Wow, that's quite the perspective. Didn't he have kids? And they lived with you?"

"Yes, and fortunately, I still have a wonderful relationship with them and their mom."

"Oh, that's great! Wow, that says a lot about her. And you. You know what, this might sound weird, but you seem different. You feel different."

"Thank you! I think?" We both laugh.

"No, in a good way. A great way!"

"I'm curious. What do you mean by that?"

"You seem less competitive. You feel more content. It's

almost like you've grown into yourself." Janet says this as she interlaces her hands and places them in her lap.

"Thank you. I really appreciate that."

"I don't know. It's almost like you seem more willing to look around you and appreciate things for what they are. I'm not sure how else to explain it."

"I think I understand what you're saying, and that truly means a lot."

We finish talking shop and part ways with a hug and a smile. I'm also smiling on the inside.

Back home at a cute little wine bar, I'm enjoying a glass of wine at happy hour with another industry colleague, Michelle. We live within a few miles of one another and wanted to catch up somewhere close to home.

I arrive first and order a meat and cheese board for us to share and a glass of wine for myself. Barely noticing that Michelle's a little late, I settle in at the booth side of the table while I wait for her to arrive. What's more notable to me is my laid-back reaction to her tardiness. I've become much more relaxed over the last few years.

After catching up on small talk, Michelle leans in a little more intensely and says to me across the table, "You feel like you've gone through such a huge transformation, Ginny."

I tilt my head a bit and reply, "You said that to me last time we got together, too, Michelle. Do you mind sharing with me what you mean by that?"

"I'll try to explain it the best I can. I'm basing it on the years I've known you and meeting you in a business setting. You used to have an energy of self-pressure and pushed yourself in the corporate world." She pauses to take a sip of wine.

Michelle continues, "That's amazing, but seeing you now, I see your passion and the light you exude is so bright. You look beautiful. I don't know if I'm explaining this very well, but you seem okay with yourself. You're still driven and an overachiever, but you do things now with love behind it. It seems like things are easier for you. You seem so much at peace. Does that make sense?" She kind of chuckles.

"Wow." I sit back in my seat. "Thank you." I think for a second about who I was even as recently as a few years ago and can see in myself that I've become more patient, less inflexible, and more open-hearted. "I'm very flattered that you would say those things about me, and I appreciate you taking the time to share your thoughts and observations with me."

Michelle raises her glass, and I meet it with mine as she says, "Cheers to transformation."

"Cheers to transformation."

BELIZE IT

I'M CROSS-LEGGED ON THE SOFA on the balcony that overlooks the turquoise waters gently dancing along the shoreline of white sand. It's breathtaking and I'm grateful to be here.

The last time I remember gazing out over the ocean was the time I was filled with sadness over losing the man I thought I knew and the family I thought I'd built.

Now, I sit here encapsulated in joy—joy for the life I've built and the person I've grown into since then. I've been able to maintain a relationship with Taylor and Logan—our modern family. After thinking I'd lost them completely, we've developed a perfect rhythm that works for us.

I'm filled with anticipation about how in the spring, Elsa and I will be embarking on a trip with them to Hawaii, where they'll see the ocean for a second time in their lives. And Elsa will get this experience with them for the first time. I'm giddy with excitement at seeing it through her eyes.

My thoughts are interrupted when I hear the sliding door behind me and Lauren pops her head out in between the crack, "Hey, what are you up to out here?"

"I'm just taking it all in. The scenery is so beautiful."

She takes a seat in a chair to join me in relishing in the last minutes of daylight.

Once dusk officially hits, Lauren says, "Should we get ready to head to dinner pretty soon?"

"Yeah, I'm right behind you." I want to absorb every last second of me and Lauren's final night of our girls trip in Belize.

I step inside to get myself presentable for dinner. As I catch a glimpse of my reflection in the glass, I can't help but smile, despite noticing my unruly hair from the heat and humidity. It's a smile of appreciation for the journey I've been on—a smile for granting that girl in the mirror a little grace—a smile for allowing myself to acknowledge the hurt and heal the pain —a smile for this new more vulnerable version of me.

I sweep the wand of color across my smiling mouth for the final touch before our last dinner of vacation. There's just one last thing I need to do before I'm ready. Staring into the mirror at my own reflection, I say aloud, "You're My Favorite."

I slide my feet into my shoes, slip my arm through the strap of my handbag and yell to Lauren, "I'm ready!"

ACKNOWLEDGMENTS

THANK YOU TO EVERYONE who in some capacity, big or small, provided inspiration, guidance, love, encouragement and support throughout this journey and process—whether you're aware of your impact or not. This includes the uber talented Rodney K Press and Albatross teams who I'm eternally grateful to for their editing and design expertise.

A special thank you to the following individuals who without their contributions this book would not have been made possible:

"Lauren" - Thank you for finding the bravery within yourself to come to me on November 13, 2018. That was a cocktail hour neither of us are bound to forget. Your strength and courage are admirable.

"Elsa" - Your grace, open-heartedness, kindness and understanding are qualities that anyone would aspire to possess. You have revealed how much I've gained along this journey through the unexpected bond we've formed. Thank you for embracing me as a part of your life and the kids' lives. I love our modern family – a chosen family.

"The kids" - Thank you for showing me that I did have it inside myself to have a positive influence as a parent figure. I can't imagine life without you in it. I'm filled with gratitude for the opportunity to continue to be a part of yours and watch you grow into adults that can contribute positively to this world.

Lindsay - Lindsay, Lindsay, Lindsay! We've laughed, we've cried, you've blushed… Oh what a ride this has been. I cannot imagine navigating this process and bringing this book and story to fruition with anyone other than you. You were the type of leader to me that I've always strived to be for others - you stretched me beyond the limits of what I believed I could have ever accomplished. Your encouragement and steadfastness got me through to the end, which is really only the beginning.

ABOUT THE AUTHOR

GINNY PRIEM is an authentic and influential leader. Throughout her career, she has honed her gift as a respected and natural speaker and presenter. With her aptitude for all forms of communication, *You're My Favorite* was created - her debut book as a published author. She is curious and passionate about personal growth and overall wellness. A Minnesota native, Ginny is a lover of travel and experiences. She continues to reside in the Minneapolis area with her Cavalier King Charles Spaniel, Francine, who is generous enough to share her king-size bed with Ginny.

For speaking engagements, author inquiries, and to download a free book discussion guide, scan the QR code below to visit *www.ginnypriem.com*

CPSIA information can be obtained
at www.ICGtesting.com
Printed in the USA
LVHW111914020422
714992LV00012B/344

9 781737 160694